"People often ask me if I
know the secret of success
and if I could tell others how
to make their dreams come true.

My answer is, you do it by working."

–Walt Disney

Other Resources by Lee Cockerell

BOOKS
Creating Magic
10 Common Sense Leadership Strategies from a Life at Disney

The Customer Rules
The 39 Essential Rules for Delivering Sensational Service

Career Magic
How to Stay on Track to Achieve a Stellar Career

SMARTPHONE APPS
Creating Magic—Leadership & Coaching on the Go!
iPhone App

TEACHER'S GUIDES
Teacher's Guide for Creating Magic
and Time Management Magic
Go to *www.LeeCockerell.com* to download and print

WEBSITES
www.LeeCockerell.com
Weekly leadership thoughts, seminars,
keynote speeches, blog & podcast

www.Thrive15.com
15-minute videos to move your life and career from
surviving to thriving (Free to veterans)

www.TheSportsMindInstitute.com
The Life Lessons of Sports—Extraordinary people
who share personal stories about their relationship
with sports well beyond the scoreboard

PODCAST *(15 minutes weekly)*
Creating Disney Magic Podcast on iTunes, iHeart Radio,
Stitcher Radio and on my website www.LeeCockerell.com

CAREER MAGIC

★ ★ ★ ★ ★

HOW TO STAY ON TRACK
TO ACHIEVE A STELLAR CAREER

LEE COCKERELL

emerge
publishing

TULSA, OKLAHOMA

20 19 18 17 16   10 9 8 7 6 5 4 3 2 1

CAREER MAGIC — How to Stay on Track to Achieve a
Stellar Career

© 2016 Lee Cockerell

Published by:
Emerge Publishing, LLC
9521B Riverside Parkway, Suite 243
Tulsa, Oklahoma 74137
Phone: 888.407.4447
www.EmergePublishing.com

Cover Design: Christian Ophus, Emerge Publishing
Interior Design: Anita Stumbo

Library of Congress Cataloging-in-Publication Data
ISBN: 978-1-943127-32-0 Hardcover
ISBN: 978-1-943127-33-7 E-book
ISBN: 978-1-943127-34-4 Audio Book (2017 release)

BISAC Category:
BUS012000 Careers / General
BUS037020 Careers / Job Hunting

Printed in Canada.

Career Magic is dedicated to Priscilla. She has put up with me for 48 years as we moved 11 times around the world searching for career magic. We finally found it right in front us when we realized the magic is family, health and happiness.

Acknowledgements

This was a fun book to write most of time, except when I was reminded of some of the real downers in my career. I owe my success to a lot of people. If you find your name in this book you were a positive influence on my career. I am sure I have forgotten many of you but I still appreciate you. And a special note of thanks to my publisher Christian Ophus, who is the founder and owner of Emerge Publishing.

Contents

FOREWORD

I N THE FALL OF **2010,** I was getting ready to deploy to Iraq for the third time, then as a 4-star general and commander of United States Forces-Iraq (USF-I). The 15-month period was shaping up to be an incredibly challenging one. The 50,000 American troops that remained in Iraq would advise, train, assist and equip the Iraqi Security Forces that were now in the lead and providing for the security of their country. At the same time, our troops would still be facing a threat from a formidable, albeit degraded adversary in Al-Qaeda. We also faced the very real possibility that the Iraqi government would not renew the U.S.-Iraq Status of Forces Agreement and we would be required to transition all military forces and equipment out of the country by the December 31, 2011, deadline (that is, in fact, what happened).

11

The scale and strategic significance of the tasks that lay before us were tremendous. I needed my leaders, both officers and non-commissioned officers—most of whom had deployed multiple times in recent years—to be ready to lead, highly motivated, and able to think creatively. The success of the mission and the lives of our troops depended upon it. And so, as I've done many times over the years, I picked up the phone and called my good friend, Lee Cockerell. I asked him if there was any chance he was available and willing to travel to Iraq to speak to the USF-I leadership. "You bet!" he told me. "Just say the word and I'll be on the next plane to Baghdad."

Soon thereafter, Lee traveled to Iraq and he spent a few days with our team at Camp Victory's Al Faw Palace. He sat and talked with young Soldiers in the chow hall, he spent time with junior officers, lieutenants, captains and majors, listening to them and learning more about the challenges they dealt with on a daily basis. He observed the close coordination that occurred between the military and members of our diplomatic corps, the embassy staff, and the 30+ nation coalition. He spoke to leaders of all ranks—Soldiers, Sailors, Airmen, Marines and Civilians—and he shared with them his key leadership strategies and principles. Every person Lee engaged walked away inspired and his positive message resonated within the command for the remainder of what was ultimately a very successful deployment.

Now, you may be asking yourself, why would a 4-star Army general call up Lee Cockerell and ask him to travel to Baghdad, Iraq to speak to a group of military leaders? Here we had a former Executive Vice President of Operations for Disney World—*"The Happiest Place On Earth!"*—giving a leadership seminar in a combat zone! I promise you, as you read this book, the answer will become as obvious to you as it was to me. Lee and I are of like minds when it comes to leadership, and he has a tremendous gift for being able to convey the principles that we both espouse in a very compelling way. I called upon Lee numerous times over the years and asked him to come and speak to my subordinate commanders and leaders. Every time he graciously agreed to do so; and, each presentation was even better than the last one.

I first met Lee back in 2000 when I attended a Strategic Leadership seminar for general officers hosted by the Chief of Staff of the Army in Orlando, Florida. Then the Executive Vice President of Operations for Walt Disney World, Lee was the final speaker on the program. By that point we had listened to numerous presentations and most of us were ready to call it a day. Then, Lee started speaking; he spoke for almost two hours—*without a single note or PowerPoint slide.* Here was a guy who had spent 30+ years in the hospitality industry, teaching general officers about leadership. Yet, when he finished, every person in the room was sitting on the edge of his or her seat. *It was "magical."*

Lee spoke to us that day with the authority that comes from experience, and with the genuine humility that defines great leaders. He also demonstrated a real passion for leadership and a clear understanding of the importance of taking care of people. In his own words: *"Management is doing things, getting things done, checking the box. Leadership is inspiring your people to accomplish the mission and taking care of them.*"

An Army veteran himself, Lee often speaks about the traits shared by effective leaders in all professions, including the military and corporate America. They include a strong commitment to teamwork and hard work, a can-do attitude, humility, a passion for learning and pursuing new opportunities, and a willingness to help others to succeed. Lee possesses an extraordinary ability to communicate his exceptional philosophy of leadership in a way that is easily embraced by others. However, it is important to note that key to the tremendous success that he has enjoyed is not the fact that he *understands* the leadership principles and techniques outlined in this book, but that he *lives by them.*

That night after the Chief of Staff of the Army's seminar had concluded, I had an opportunity to visit one of the Disney Theme Parks. I made a point to stop in several of the shops and I asked some of the cast members if they knew who Lee Cockerell was; I asked if they were familiar with his *Great Leader Strategies* which have been used to train and develop thousands of managers at the Walt Disney World® Resort. Every person I spoke with responded enthusiastically in the affirmative. They described Lee as a caring leader, present and engaged; they loved working for him. One cast member told me, "Mr. Cockerell isn't just a boss, he's an inspiring leader who takes the time to teach and develop the people who work for him." That was high praise, very well deserved. Most importantly, I believe every leader should aspire to be viewed in such a way by the people they have the good fortune to lead.

In this book, Lee takes us on a personal journey that starts with his humble beginnings in Oklahoma. Through hard work, trial and error, and persistence, he became an enormously successful and highly respected senior leader in the hospitality industry and eventually in the Walt Disney Company. He shares with his readers many of the lessons learned over the course of his extraordinary career, so that they and others may benefit from those same lessons.

Once I began reading this book I could not put it down. As a senior leader who has led troops in very challenging situations in peacetime and in combat, I can personally attest to the tremendous value of Lee's leadership philosophy. The genuine enthusiasm with which he conveys his message is both inspiring and infectious. I am confident, if you follow Lee's lessons, you too will create magic in your career!

Enjoy the journey!

GENERAL LLOYD J. AUSTIN III
U.S. Army (Ret.)

INTRODUCTION

IT WAS NOT DISNEY MAGIC that made my career so successful, *but the way I dealt with the ups and downs that made it
magical.* It will be the same with your career. Throughout
life it's not what happens to you, but how you react to what
happens, that makes the difference.

When I was the executive vice president of operations for
the Walt Disney World® Resort, I decided to write about my
own career, how it developed over time, what I learned and
how I dealt with each experience along the way.

My career was like an exciting *roller coaster* ride. There were
calm periods when I was slowly going up the track and there
were scary periods when I was careening straight down and
around some very frightening twists and turns.

I've had every career experience you can imagine; from being a private in the U.S. Army to my first job without a college degree; from being fired to being passed over while pursuing my dream job and finally receiving the most magical job in the world. After all of that, I'm having more fun and success in retirement than should be legal.

I was moved to write about my career when I was at Disney in order to help young people on the Disney College Program gain an understanding of the twists and turns careers can take. I wanted them to know they can not only survive during these transitions, but thrive as well. Careers can go off the track at any time in life, whether you're 22, 42 or 62 years old. My own career was a series of ups, downs, and transitions. The ups were fantastic and the downs were painful, even downright depressing a time or two.

I experienced times of calm and times of sudden, steep falls. During these times, the important thing to remember is that if you stay positive and understand all obstacles in life are momentary, then all you'll have to do is raise your arms, enjoy the ride and climb aboard the next coaster no matter how frightening it may seem. If you do that, I know you'll get back on track and be just fine.

I am now semi-retired from corporate life, my career is better than ever and I am having the ride of my life, with my arms high in the air.

The key to career development is recognizing what you learn along the way that prepares you for the next step. No matter what position you hold, you have an opportunity to learn a lot if you pay attention, ask questions and have a passion for your chosen career.

People are always asking me things like, "How can I get ahead? How can I get into management? How can I get promoted? How can I make more money?"

These are interesting questions, here's what I think. "I don't know exactly how you can do this, but what I can tell you is what I did and how it played out." Remember, I am taking a backward look at what I did along the way to try to figure out what I did that probably contributed to the success I have had in my career and in my personal life.

One thing you need to understand is that I am sharing advice with you on how I did it because that is all I know. Advice is just that, advice, so don't blame me if you follow my advice and things don't work out. Twenty five years from now don't say, *"This is all Lee's fault. I followed his advice and it did not work out."*

This is what worked for me, and I hope you will be able to take away a few learning's to help you as you make those critical career decisions when things are going well and when they are not going so well. *Think of every obstacle in your life as a detour and not as a dead-end street.*

I suggest you solicit several points of view on this subject of career development and then develop your own plan based on what you believe will work for you. Although you can't plan for every situation, you can anticipate what could happen with your career and prepare a response should this happen. Reflection and anticipation are two very powerful methods for learning how you can do anything better and what obstacles to look out for in the future.

I think you will begin to see a trend in the traits of successful people in the business world. I say business world because that is only one measurement of success … if *you* want that kind of success. The most important thing in life and the real measure of success is: *Are you happy and healthy and are your loved ones happy? This Is Real Success!*

People with great career success, who've measured by the position they've achieved and money they've made, have only accomplished a very minute part of the definition of success. I know many individuals with big jobs and big titles whose personal lives are a mess. Many are not healthy and many are struggling with their marriages or children. I don't consider them successful in any sense of the word. Being wealthy with a big title and happiness are two completely different things. What you do and who you are, are not the same.

My recommendations in this book are the same ones I gave my son, Daniel and other people close to me over the years. Making difficult decisions and taking risks are part of the development process for careers—and life in general. Everything from accepting a new role to relocating for work; from leaving a position to going back to school can be in the equation. *Living a life without taking risks is a shame.* Don't be so careful that you end up with lots of regrets one day. Living on the edge is where the fun is!

First things first. When you think that you are running out of time and you need to pick up the pace, keep in mind that most of us will work 45–50 years. *Fast experience is not always the best experience and it's not only the experience that counts.* What you learn from that experience and how you apply it toward becoming excellent is what really matters.

Good luck!

1

IN THE BEGINNING
1964–1969

I N THIS CHAPTER, I am going to tell you about a couple of jobs in my career, what I learned, and how they eventually helped me get to where I am today. This might be helpful to those of you out there who think all of the good jobs are gone.

The key is making sure that you are taking advantage of each experience in order to gain maximum knowledge as well as building a strong foundation and relationships so that you'll be successful in each role. Excellence is always recognized because so many people don't operate in it.

The real key is always going above and beyond. If ten people do what you do, you make sure you are the best; from a can do attitude and passion to knowledge and skill to reliability and performance.

I held 22 "real jobs" throughout my career before retiring from Disney in 2006 to start my own company and I must say, I was the best performer, going above and beyond in each one of those positions, in my humble opinion. I believed I was the best because I was so insecure that I just worked harder than everyone else. My biggest fear was fear of failure and I used it in my favor.

I say "real jobs" because I define real as full-time. These are the kind of jobs that pay the rent and put food on the table. I had five part-time jobs before these real jobs, but I still had my mom as a backup since I lived at home while I had them. Those part time jobs don't count as much as the real ones—wherein if you don't perform, you don't eat.

I believe I achieved success in my career through a combination of:

- Taking risks,
- Gaining a lot of varied experiences,
- Having patience,
- Being better and trying harder than everyone else at every job,
- Being committed to the job (time on the job each day including six day workweeks, improving self-awareness and learning from my mistakes),
- And most of all, having a very positive attitude, which I will explain next. I was also fortunate to have two

great mentors along the way who took a personal interest in this area of my development.

One of the key factors in my success, I believe, is because I am wired to be positive and in a good mood even under stress. I am disciplined and well organized, too. I have a good sense of humor, and I have loved all of my jobs for the most part. If you are disciplined, organized, and have a positive attitude, you can make it easily I've found. In fact, with these attributes, you can get by for a while not even knowing what you are doing. These attributes give you the time to learn. We all give breaks to people with a positive attitude who are giving their best and trying hard.

The one thing I believe about career development is that everything must be done with excellence and your talents will stand out and be recognized. So, my advice? Be Great!

- Do great work, period! And don't be a whiner and have an excuse for everything.
- Be positive, and do what needs to be done.
- Become an expert.
- Make your boss look good.
- Don't be a person who creates problems and extra work for your boss.
- Be organized and reliable. You may want to read my book *Time Management Magic: How To Get More Done Every Day and Move From Surviving to Thriving.*

Okay, so that is the first bit of advice for creating *Career Magic!*

I went to college for two years and made pretty bad grades. I don't learn well in the classroom. I learn best by doing and then by teaching others what I have learned. I guess if my parents had bought me *Hooked on Phonics, Hooked on Math,* and *Hooked on Doing Your Homework* or *How To Be A Great Student for Dummies,* I would have done better in school—but one rule I have is, *you can't blame your parents for the mess you put yourself in.* I was "Hooked on Fun," and "hooked on fun" does not prepare you for the real world, as I later found out.

I was born in Bartlesville, Oklahoma, and grew up on a dairy farm near Copan, Oklahoma. We were very poor. Our house did not even have indoor plumbing. We had an outhouse for a toilet and my mother heated water on the stove and bathed my brother Jerry and me in a big tub in the kitchen. I attended the Antioch one room schoolhouse with grades one through eight in one room with one teacher for eight grades. There was a second room for grades nine through twelve with another teacher. My mother was married five times. I was adopted twice and am on my third name since birth. I received the name Cockerell when I was 16 years old. The odds of becoming the head of Disney World Operations in the future was pretty near zero. The lesson? *Never underestimate what you can achieve.*

My first job at eight-years-old was to milk a dairy cow by hand every morning before going to school. We had electric milking machines, but my parents gave me this job for development, I suppose. I put on a pair of white overalls every morning over my school clothes (cows don't take a day off) and milked my cow and sold the milk for 50¢ to our neighbors, the Thompsons that lived across the road. Mr. and Mrs. Thompson had a peach orchard and gave me fresh peaches during the summer. That was my first job, and I was already learning about perks. Fresh peaches are a nice perk when you are eight and 50¢ was big money. On another note, I have yet to find peaches that taste as good as those did when I was eight.

You may be saying right now, "Why is Lee telling us all of this? What does all of this have to do with *career development?*" Your work matters at every level! The discipline I learned when I was eight has contributed to the work ethic I've had ever since!

Many parents are not giving their children enough routine, increasing responsibility and holding them accountable for completing it. I think learning good work habits early, is vital. Make sure your children have lots of responsibility until they are old enough to get a job. Priscilla and I made sure our son, Daniel worked in the summers and he and his wife Valerie have made sure their children work during the summer while having responsibilities in the home as well.

My brother, Jerry and I sat on the back of my grandfather's hay baler in the summers and made sure the bales of hay were tied properly while my grandfather drove the tractor. We thought this was fun. We cleaned up the barn after the cows had been milked. We didn't think this was fun—except throwing dried cow manure at each other. That was fun … *unless you were hit in the face.*

After 5th grade we moved to Ardmore, Oklahoma, where

my dad began a large trucking company to supply the thriving oil business. We were still poor, but things were a bit better and now we had indoor plumbing.

My next part-time job was working in a lumberyard when I was 16 and in tenth grade. I was a minor, but that didn't seem to matter as much in those days. We unloaded train cars of cement, sheet rock, and lumber. The pay was $1 per hour. The work was hard and hot, and I was sure this was not what I wanted to do for the rest of my life. I became physically fit, though. Being in the top of a boxcar in August is an experience you will never forget.

My mother worked full-time as a bookkeeper so she taught my brother and I to do the house chores. We were expected to clean the house, do the dishes by hand, laundry our clothes, iron them and do the yard work.

My mother didn't mess around. If we did not do our chores and do them well she was very clear with us about what would happen. Our punishment would include more than just a "timeout" or taking our cell phones away—obviously there were no cell phones and even if there had been, we couldn't afford one. We got our first television when I was in the fifth grade so we had plenty of time to do house chores growing up. My mother had a great incentive program; when you finish your chores, you can play. That system always helped us focus and move quicker to complete our work.

Priscilla and I made sure our son Daniel had these same hard-work experiences by working on a cattle ranch in Oklahoma during the hot summers, clearing brush and digging fence postholes. Daniel made sure his son Jullian had a similar opportunity. Jullian worked in horticulture for two summers pulling weeds and spreading hundreds of bags of mulch from 6:00am–2:00pm in 90 degree heat. He learned a lot about being on time, working with others and following instructions.

The horticulture company calls it "The Stay in School Program." I believe it helped him when he headed off to college at 17 and had to have the discipline to get up early and get to class on his own. Many parents are not preparing their children by giving them increasing levels of responsibility, subjecting them to hard work and holding them accountable. My mother wasn't moved if we weren't happy every minute of every day, but she focused on preparing us to be successful. My brother became a surgeon and I ended up running Disney World Operations. Do this for your children and you will have given them the best gift in the world, self-reliance! They will thank you one day.

My next job was in eleventh grade, delivering prescriptions for Park's Drug Store. I wrecked the brand new delivery car the day it was purchased because I was looking down at my paperwork instead of looking at the road. The owner of the drug store, Henry Parks was very kind and understanding and did not fire me. He told me to go home and take a nap. I will never forget how understanding and kind he was—and how scared I was. *The lesson is not to overreact to things. You might do permanent harm to someone's self-confidence and self-esteem, especially a young person.* At this job I also worked the soda fountain, sold food and even helped out selling merchandise in the store between deliveries. This was my first food, beverage and retail experience. Serving customers was far different than cleaning up barn stalls and unloading lumber. The perk here was air conditioning.

My next part-time job was in college where I was a kitchen steward in the SAE fraternity house at Oklahoma State University. I worked in the kitchen and dining room. I learned a lot about food preparation, serving, how to be on time and to work as a team. I remember I was serving dinner on October 22, 1962, when President Kennedy came on TV to tell us that he was putting a naval blockade around Cuba and would use military force if necessary. This was the beginning of the Cuban Missile Crisis, which lasted 13 days. I thought of JFK and this incident often throughout my career when I had tough decisions to make as a leader, which made my issues seem like child's play compared with dealing with Nikita Khrushchev and the chances of starting a nuclear war.

My next job at 19 was working in the Oklahoma oil fields and living away from home for the summer vacation after my freshman year at college. I rented a room in a boarding house and worked in the oil fields helping to repair natural gas pipelines and in a refinery cleaning motors in the 100-degree Oklahoma heat. The men who I worked with were tough and actually ate whole raw onions with their sandwiches at lunch, while smoking a cigarette at the same time. They didn't care too much for the young college kids, but by the end of the summer, they liked me. Maybe it was because I was now eating a raw onion with my lunch too. I learned to keep fairly quiet in that job and just do what I was told. I think those oilmen liked that and tolerated me for it, which seemed to be the highest accolade achievable among them.

My final part-time job after my second year at Oklahoma State was working at Harvey's Wagon Wheel Hotel and Casino in Lake Tahoe, Nevada. My first job that summer was working as a "Grease Man." It paid $2.25 per hour. That job consisted of pushing a little cart around all of the kitchens and emptying the grease from the griddles that built up as the cooks grilled hamburgers, bacon, and so forth. I can tell you that the job as Grease Man was not a highly respected job by the other employees, but that's where they made a mistake. It taught me to *always remember that everyone is important. This one thing will enhance your career dramatically.*

I earned $90 a week in this job and lost it all every week playing Blackjack in Harrah's Casino after work as there was really nothing else to do.

My second job that summer was working in housekeeping on the night shift. My job was to do turndown service which included turning down the beds, tidying up the room and cleaning the bathrooms.

One night playing Blackjack at Harrah's Casino a security officer approached me and asked to see my ID to check my age. I showed him my fake driver's license and was asked me to sign my name the way it appeared on the ID. Of course I couldn't do that and was promptly handcuffed and put into jail for four hours until my roommates could round up $100 to bail me out. I went to court the next morning and the judge fined me $25 and returned $75 to me. He told me and the other forty under age gamblers in the court room that he better not see us again this summer. My gambling days were over. Going forward my gambling consisted mainly of accepting career moves which sometimes had risky odds.

Thinking back about those early days reminded me how some of the managers I worked with would not treat everyone respectfully because of the position they held or where they were from. I asked someone just the other day, "Who do you think is more important, the person who orders the French fries, the person who stores them properly right away in the freezer, the person who delivers them, the person who cooks and salts them, the person who serves them, the person who cleans them off the dining room table, or the person who sweeps them off the floor?" One of the most important things I learned during all these early jobs was that, everyone's important and that you better respect them or you will be doing all of these jobs by yourself when they all quit.

You don't last long without your team.

I dropped out of college after two years and entered the U.S. Army in 1964. (This is not the same advice I gave my son). This was pretty common in our family. I was the first in my family to go to college. My brother was the first to finish and as I told you before, he became an orthopedic surgeon. For fun I often tell people that if I had finished college, I would have had a really good job too. This does annoy some college graduates so I don't use that sort of humor too often, especially with Ivy League graduates, many of whom have worked for me over the years. I also had a nice perk having no college loans to pay off.

When I got on that bus in Ardmore in September 1964 to report to Fort Polk in Leesville, Louisiana, for basic training, my mother was crying. She later told me she had almost died the day I was born and almost died again the day I got on that bus to go into the Army. I was on my way to the scary real world, and she knew it! I didn't know it at the time, but soon learned why she was crying so.

I went to cook school in the Army and out of a class of several hundred cooks; I placed second in my class just below a professional cook from England by the name of Terrence Biggs. I learned quickly on the job. I hadn't had much cooking experience, I could read the recipes, and I knew how to follow instructions. If you think Army food is bad, you don't know how badly it can be if you don't follow the recipes. In fact Army food is quite good. Don't believe everything you hear.

There are different levels of good and bad. *I learned to have a great respect for following instructions.* Once I made dough for 300 hamburger buns but did not pay attention to when and how to add the yeast. I won't tell you the whole story, but I can tell you I had a bad day. I was lucky not to be court-martialed for ruining all of those ingredients.

For the next few days, I was assigned dishwashing and potato peeling since the automatic potato peeling machines were not working. I peeled those potatoes faster than anyone ever had, and I did it with a good attitude; soon I got my cook's job back. *When you have a setback you need to stay positive and work your way back up, learning from that mistake. A mistake repeated is a decision.* A bad attitude and poor performance will get you nothing but trouble, and take you nowhere fast.

I learned that if I am allowed to do something, and someone shows me how to do it, then I could do it. That was a good lesson in self-awareness, which may be one of the most important traits a leader can have.

I met two Brits in the Army, Graham Cromack and Terrence Biggs. These were the first foreigners I had ever met. In those days if you were in the US on a green card you had to serve in the military.

When I was discharged from the Army, I went to Washington, D.C. with Terrence Biggs, the professional cook who had beat me out of placing first in cook's school. Spend time with the number one if possible, as you can learn from them. *Knowing the right people doesn't hurt! In fact having good relationships with others will be a major factor in your career success.* Graham and I got an apartment together.

Terrence told me he was going to be the chef at the Washington Hilton that was opening in three weeks and that he would get me a job too. I was 20 years old so what was there to lose? It sounded good to me. I thought I might as well take a risk. What's the worst thing that can happen to you when you are twenty? Going into the Army was the second time I had ever stepped foot out of Oklahoma since I was born and going to Washington, D.C., was the third. My second time was a day trip to Dallas, just 90 miles from my home in Ardmore when I was 19.

We stopped in Ardmore, picked up my car and drove across country for two days arriving in Washington, D.C. on March 1 and checked into the Twin Bridges Marriott Hotel in Virginia. Marriott Hotels even then were ahead of their time. They had drive-in check-in and you didn't even have to get out of your car. The room was eight dollars a night. Marriott had about twelve hotels in 1964. I had never heard of them. I thought at that time that Marriott was just a little nothing hotel company. Boy was I wrong! Marriott years later became an important part of my career. They had 32 hotels in 1964. Never underestimate what you can achieve. Today Marriott has over four thousand hotels.

Terrence and I went over to the Washington Hilton the next day, and it turns out that my buddy Terrence was actually going to be the room service breakfast cook and not the chef. *The lesson here is don't believe everything everyone tells you. Many people enhance their résumé titles I have learned.* All stories sound true in isolation of the other side of the story. I use that lesson today almost every day. As they say, "trust but verify." An applicant once listed on his application that he had worked for the government for two years. That turned out to be true. He was in prison those two years.

The Washington Hilton was in utter turmoil as it was just two weeks from the grand opening. The lady in the employment office said, "So what do you want to do? What job do you want?"

I looked at her with a blank stare because I had no idea what I wanted to do because I had never been in a hotel in my life, except a couple of cheesy motels with ten rooms. I had never really been to a nice restaurant where they had linen napkins and more than one fork, one knife, and one spoon so I was pretty taken back by her question even though I should have anticipated it. In my house you licked off the dinner fork to eat your pie and there were no dishwashers back then, except my brother and myself.

I regained my composure and through some quick thinking I told her I would like to be a room service waiter as I had seen on television movies, and had noticed these waiters would get tipped in cash. I did not have a credit card, so cash seemed like a pretty good idea. I also learned during the last stock market plunge why people say, "Cash is King!" I wish I had learned that lesson earlier, but now I will always remember it. *Experience causes you to think differently, you see.* Reading about stock-market declines and experiencing it with your own money are two different things. Reading about other people losing their money is not very emotional. Losing your own money is very emotional!

The personnel manager said, "No, the room service jobs are all filled already you can be a banquet waiter." I agreed not quite knowing what that meant. The only banquet I had ever been to was my high-school prom dinner, and that was in the YWCA basement in Ardmore.

After being hired I walked into the Grand Ballroom of the hotel and almost had a heart attack. It seated three thousand guests, they told me. I still have no idea why they gave me that job. The only experience I had was that I was a kitchen steward in my fraternity house in college serving 25–40 people at a time. I guess a little experience is better than no experience at all. *All experience is valuable and you never know when it will pay off.* I did list my food serving experience from my fraternity house on the application as well as my food and beverage experience from the Army. When you're young many employers will turn you down because of lack of experience so get every bit you can.

I had no clue about how to be a professional waiter, but I was lucky. One of the banquet supervisors, Kurt, a German fellow, took me under his wing and told me to pay attention and he would train me, and everything would be fine. I loved this man instantly. *We all need to look for opportunities to help others.* None of us had experience before we had experience so give people a break when you can especially if they have a can do, positive attitude and passion. I call those, high potential people. The only thing they're missing is skill and that can be acquired with training.

If it had not been for Kurt, I don't know where I would be today. His training really helped me to become successful. *If you are a leader, your job is to develop others.* Be like Kurt.

First, I learned all of those fancy napkin folds and how to skirt a table without clip-on skirting because it had not been invented yet. We skirted tables with tablecloths and without pins. You had to learn how to fold the cloths just so they would perfectly drop a half-inch from the floor. This is hard to do. I learned where the glasses went, in which order, and into which glasses to pour the wines and the water.

Even today I use what I learned in that job. Priscilla, and I can have 50 people to our house for dinner and do it all by ourselves—without any help or a catering company helping us. That position has helped me a lot and saved me plenty of money over the years.

From there it was progressive training, observing, practicing, and most of all making mistakes and learning from them. *I asked a lot of questions,* since I had never seen most of the food that was served. At least it was not prepared and displayed that way back home in Oklahoma by my mom or the local restaurants. I ate my first lamb, oyster, snail, and flaming cherries for the Baked Alaska ice cream bombs, which I definitely never had in Oklahoma. Whoever heard of baking ice cream?

I was always cooperative. When one of my many bosses wanted someone to stay late or open early, my hand went up. This paid off later. All of my bosses through the years liked that, too. Some things never change. People want to work with those who are willing to go the extra mile, have a good work ethic, and a good attitude.

I learned this job well and, if I do say so myself, became an excellent banquet server. I served Lyndon Johnson, President of the United States, at one dinner on the head table and also Senator Ted Kennedy breakfast while he was still in a wheelchair from a plane crash he had been in earlier in 1964. I served so many famous people that I cannot even start to remember them all. Some were nice and gracious, and some were not. This, too, was a good lesson that would serve me well later in my career. *Be nice to people was a lesson in and of itself.*

Don't get too big for your britches, as my mother would often say. I assure you that humility will serve you well. When you are a big deal, don't be!

I learned how to serve food and beverage, all about wines and the service of wines, how to carve anything and everything. I learned how to open oysters. I learned Russian service, French service, and good old American plate service. I learned how to be a bartender. I learned how to carry on brief conversations with famous people and those who thought they were famous. I learned how to be professional in my personal appearance and to polish my shoes at the risk of being sent home. I learned to appreciate my fellow workers who were from every country in the world. This experience taught me many lessons about the importance of diversity, which I hadn't had the opportunity of learning while growing up in Oklahoma. I learned how to work hard, every hour even during long and continual shifts. Often I was already at work come 5:00am usually there until midnight, then back again for breakfast the next day. Even through those long days I learned how remain professional, friendly, and courteous. Stay fit; high energy and stamina matter and will help you be successful and help you deal with stress

This experience showed me the other side of what goes on behind the scenes; the theft of products by my fellow workers, ways of deceiving the boss, and the ways to make the guest's checks larger so the tips would increase.

I observed so called leaders misbehaving and watched them do things that were against the policy of the company—or, at a minimum, poor judgment. Their mothers would not have been happy with their behaviors. I did not have respect for many of them. I don't ever want to forget this lesson when I deal with people and as I tell people today in my books and seminars, *"Be careful what you say and do as everyone is always watching you and judging you."* Your reputation is at stake every second of every day. Value it and protect it. One mistake these days can find its way to the internet and do permanent damage to your career.

I experienced bosses and guests treating me as if I was nobody. I experienced bosses that never asked my opinion and who set a very poor example. I never once, ever, saw the general manager of the hotel. I don't think he was comfortable in behind the scene areas. I worked with a lot of "managers" who did not understand the responsibility and meaning of leadership and being a good role-model

What are these experiences worth, you might say? I would tell you that you couldn't buy this course in college. I know this because I had been to college and these types of experiences were not there. The education you receive from experience doesn't only go into your head, but it goes into your heart—never to be forgotten! They wait there until you need them sometime in the future. *Experience helps your intuition and judgment considerably.* Today's young people do not want theory. They want reality. College gives you theory. Experience gives you reality. Get both.

I know things that some people will never know. I was able to see things in this serving job that some people will never see. I saw and did things in this job at the young age of 20 that have helped me become a better manager and leader ever since. *This experience helped me to know when I was doing it right and when I was doing it wrong.*

The positive side of this job was that I made a lot of money. This was 1965 and I was earning $13,000 in nine months and then taking the summer off to go to the beach in Atlantic City. The downside was that I worked day and night. In those days our schedule was posted only three days in advance, so it was difficult to plan anything in advance for travel or recreation. Like every job there, it came with both the good and the bad. Let me remind you that *every job has good things and things that are not so good. Such is life. There are good days and bad days.*

I learned about unions and was a member of the Hotel Employees and Restaurant Employees Union (HERE). I have been on both sides and understand clearly the position of each. This definitely helped a great deal later on in my career when I was involved in union negotiations as an executive at Disney. Don't underestimate the importance of understanding the people on the other side and the art of compromise.

The summers were not as busy in large convention hotels so I would take the summer off. The first summer I went to Atlantic City. This was long before any casinos were there. Atlantic City was very nice. I loved the boardwalk and the beach. As soon as I arrived in Atlantic City, I found a room at the Kentucky Hotel for ten dollars a week. This place was scary and would have surely burned down in 60 seconds if there were a fire. Next, I started looking for a job. I found one rather quickly at Luigi's Italian restaurant on Pacific Avenue. I got the job because of my experience of being a waiter at the Washington Hilton. As I said before, all experience has value. This was one of the best summers of my life. I worked five days a week from 4:00pm–9:00pm and had fun the other 19 hours of the day. I will keep those stories to myself. I made between twenty five to thirty dollars in cash tips every night. Back in those days hardly anyone paid with a credit card.

Again, I learned a lot. Being a banquet server is different than being a restaurant server and I learned all about Italian food. The owner provided meals to all employees, but the only item we could have was spaghetti and tomato sauce with Italian bread. We were not allowed to ever have meat sauce or meatballs so I had the same meal, every day for three months. After a few weeks I moved in with 20 other young people is a big house on Atlantic Avenue where we each paid ten dollars per week. The house was great. There was a 24-hour poker game going on in the kitchen the whole summer in which I did not participate after my gambling problem in Lake Tahoe the summer before.

I think every young person should try to get a server's job. It teaches you to be organized and composed while quickly thinking on your feet and at the same time, serving all kinds of people. Some leave big tips and some leave nothing. When Daniel was old enough we made sure he had a server's job at Phillip's Crab House in Ocean City, Maryland and when our grandson Jullian was old enough he was a server as well. This is one of the best jobs in the world for introverts. You start as an introvert in June and by the end of the summer you're an extrovert.

After the summer ended in September, I headed back to the Washington Hilton to return to my full time job serving banquets. After a few months however, I decided that I wanted to get an office job and have more consistency in my schedule, weekends off, and go home at 5:00pm I heard about a position that was available in the food and beverage accounting department, but it was a clerical job. I applied and was turned down because I didn't have any experience in that line of work. I told the manager of the department that I had taken accounting twice in college, but that wasn't enough to impress him one bit.

About two months later the food control manager came looking for me and asked me if I still wanted the job. I said, "Yes." I thought that I had just gotten my big break, but it turned out he offered me the job because he couldn't find anyone else to take it for the salary of $80 a week. At the time I was making several times that as a banquet server.

Since I was single I figured I would find a way to make this low salary work. My rent was $52 a month, just down the street from the Hilton and I got most of my meals free at the hotel. *If you want experience, you often have to pay the price.* Don't worry about how much you make when you are young, instead worry about how much you need to make when you are old.

I accepted the food and beverage control position, but soon also had to get a job as a waiter in a French restaurant at night in order to be able to afford my apartment, car payments and frequent trips to the discos and restaurants in Georgetown. My recreation expenses were high. I was rarely off at 5:00pm and being off on weekends never happened. I worked six nights a week as a waiter and Monday through Friday in the clerk's job. I did get every Sunday off, so that was a little better. The upside? *I learned how to be a restaurant server in an upscale restaurant,* which was far different than being a banquet server. So, now I had another experience under my belt, which would pay off later in my career when I became a restaurant manager.

I learned a lot during my time as the clerk at the food control job. My boss was "Mr. Organized." He had a daily minute-by-minute schedule for me taped on the wall next to my desk and I had to follow that schedule to the minute.

- 8:00–8:15: Go to chef's office and pick up food-transfer forms
- 8:15–8:45: Price out transfer forms
- 8:45–9:00: Go to food storeroom and collect food requisitions from the day before
- 9:00–10:00: Price out food requisitions
- 10:00–10:15: Break
- 10:15–11:00: Price out beverage requisitions
- 11:00–11:30: Audit each invoice for accuracy
- 11:30–12:00: Do inventory of room service bar
- 12:00–1:00 Lunch

This is how the whole day went, minute to minute until

5:00pm This guy was tough, but this is where I learned how effective checklists could be. I love checklists today just as much as I have since I learned this early lesson. You have to understand that electronic calculators were not even invented yet, let alone cell phones with task list capability. We had these huge manual calculator machines with paper tape that would do basic math, but they were slow.

My boss taught me a lot about accounting systems, how to analyze the Profit & Loss (P&L) statements and how to do unit P&Ls using a model for how to allocate non-direct costs. He was French; and when we took the inventory of the wines at the end of each month, he would make me call out the names of each of the wines, which in those days were mainly French wines in the big hotels and fancy restaurants. He made me call them out for two reasons. The first reason was that he wanted me to learn how to pronounce them, and the second reason was that it made him laugh when this Oklahoma boy did attempt to pronounce them. After he had finally stopped laughing he took the time to explain each region where the wines were from. He taught me a lot and I'm grateful for his instruction so that when I lived in France 23 years later I could pronounce the wines when I went out to dinner. My French is poor but I can still pronounce French wines properly.

I gained a lot from this position. The experiences were wonderful. *Looking back I had not earned a lot, but I learned a lot and it was worth it.* As you can see, if you remove the "L" from learned, you have the word earned and that's how you should think about experiences. What did you walk away with that is yours to keep forever and use later, even as a gift to others? When you have done the job yourself, your credibility increases dramatically with those you lead.

You should learn new things every day in every position you hold. This is a sure fire way of both not getting bored and preparation for the next opportunity.

I often heard the college program cast members at Disney World saying that they couldn't learn anything in the jobs we assigned them. I know that this is not true. In every job, you can learn a lot if you are paying attention, asking questions, and have a desire to learn. Today you have no excuse for not learning, you have Google at your fingertips.

Just remember that every experience in life can be a good experience in one way or another if you choose to see it that way. The things I learned from these first three jobs were extremely valuable and continue to serve me well today. *My pay was low, but I had already earned a million dollars worth of experience.*

Next I'll review my following two jobs, after becoming the best food control clerk I could be, and will show you how I earned $2 million in experience!

2

MARRIAGE, BABY, MANAGEMENT & THE BIG APPLE

1968–1969

WITH MY FIRST MILLION of experience earned in the last three jobs, what do I do with it? I decided just to invest it in more experience to try to leverage that first million in experience into several million more.

As one of my bosses told me way back, *"Lee, worry about the job you have and not the one you want."*

He was saying that it's better to do a great job with the role you have or you won't ever have to worry about the next job.

He also meant stay focused, and be the best that you can be in every way including attitude, professional appearance, work ethic, quality of work, timeliness, communication, continuous learning, and so on. Do this and the next job will arrive.

When you do a great job, it doesn't take long before someone notices because so many are doing just enough to get by.

Remember that the purpose of this book is to give everyone some food for thought. If you can begin to think differently, you can begin to act and perform differently. With some self-awareness, drive, continuous learning, commitment, and a little patience I know that if you can dream it, you can achieve it and as Walt Disney said himself, *"If you can dream it, you can do it."*

I continue to make the point that *in every single experience you have, you can learn something that you can use in the future.* Begin now to think about every experience as an opportunity to learn.

I am not telling you that while I was in some of my positions back then I felt this way. I, like many people, did not understand the value of experience and how it educates you in a special and lasting way. I know it now, though. You can learn from others who have been there. If I sound like your mom and dad, I am sorry, but it is the truth. Your parents teach this and harp on it because they love you and I do it because I want you to have a magical, exciting, and fulfilling career.

Looking back, some of my worst jobs, worst bosses, and worst circumstances turned out to be some of my most valuable experiences. Remember, I said *looking back.* When I was back there in those days, I did not always feel that I was getting good experience. I sometimes felt like I was getting the raw end of the deal and should have never taken that job. I felt underpaid, underappreciated and overworked. Have you ever felt that way? If you say no, you are a very lucky person, so count your blessings.

Careers, like roller coasters, don't always go straight up. They go up and down, and after a while you learn that *the scary downs are temporary as long as you stay positive.* With determination, you will keep going up even though from time to time you may have an upset stomach and wish the ride were over.

Sometimes these negative experiences are called things such as, bad luck, personality clash, wrong place at the wrong time, not fair, and many other things. I can tell you that I have had several ups and downs in my career. You will learn more about them in the next few chapters. Maybe hearing my story will help you avoid some of these same career mistakes and hazards.

When one of these negative situations happen, it's imperative that you *pick yourself up and get going again.* Hopefully, you will have learned from each experience so that the same thing doesn't continue happening over and over. As I said earlier, a mistake repeated is a decision.

In the first chapter, I talked about my first three real, full-time jobs. The first was as a cook in the U.S. Army, the second was as a banquet server, and the third was a clerk in the food and beverage control office of the Washington Hilton Hotel, a very large convention hotel in Washington, D.C. This is the hotel where John Hinckley shot President Reagan on March 30, 1981. What's really weird is that John Hinckley was born in Ardmore, Oklahoma where I grew up. My career turned out better than his.

Looking back I learned more in those first three jobs than I ever imagined I would have at the time I was doing each of them. If you are reading this, please remember that *every* experience counts!

Now, for my next two positions ...

I had been the food and beverage control clerk for about eight months when the company decided to expand the role of food and beverage controller and to have one of these positions in every Hilton Hotel around the world. Well, there I was when they started looking for management trainees to train and develop for this new role. I now had the experience and I had done a great job as a clerk, so I was selected for the management-training program. Taking a low paying clerk job was paying off. *Sometimes you just have to take a lower level job to get your foot in the door so you can show how great you are.*

I was sent to Chicago for a week's worth of classroom training to learn the technical aspects of this new role. The classes were held at the Palmer House Hotel, one of the most famous Hilton Hotels. I came back to Washington, D.C., after the training and was assigned to the position of assistant food and beverage controller. I was not yet in charge of this department as the food and beverage controller, but I had my foot in the door—and that was half the battle.

No one reported to me, but who cares? I had a business card with what I thought was a nice title and it impressed some of the ladies at the nightclubs I frequented in Georgetown. Receiving a business card was one of the highlights of my early career at that time. Don't underestimate the value of the little things for your employees.

This new position was classified as management and entitled me to work many more hours than when I was the clerk and wasn't able to receive any overtime. There were no exempt and non-exempt positions back in those days.

I was working day and night and had to give up my job as a waiter in the French restaurant so I was able to continue being in this new salaried role.

I picked up work as a part-time banquet waiter. I was allowed to work serving banquet lunches on my lunch hour at the Hilton even though I was a manager in the hotel. I also worked some evenings when I was available as an on call waiter. My nightly trips to the discos in Georgetown took a dramatic reduction. There is always a way to make money if you really want to.

Yes! Back in those days, your lunch hour was an hour in length—the good old days, I guess. Can you imagine that as a salaried person I was allowed to work banquets as a waiter in the middle of my management workday for extra money? The good old days, without all of those government and company rules we have today that say what you can and cannot do on duty and off duty. Between the government, HR departments and the legal department, the good old days are long gone and many people are poorer and less well off because of so many legal rules and laws today that limit their earnings.

Well, as you know, time moves on and it wasn't long before my boss resigned, went back to France and I was promoted to his job. Something always seems to happen if you prepare yourself and hang in there.

I now had two people reporting to me. I still had only received technical training. Not one person had ever mentioned management or leadership to me in the context of what's important! I was given a new business card that read, food and beverage controller. I loved that card and promptly sent my mother and grandmother a whole stack of them to give out to their friends to prove I was making progress.

I did okay with the management part of my new job as food and beverage controller, which was mostly administrative responsibilities and bookkeeping to keep food and beverage costs under control. Between making out more checklists for everyone and a good trace system, I looked like I knew what I was doing. I had never been trained in my responsibilities as a leader so upon reflection, I believe I did well. I treated my staff with *respect,* was pretty flexible in meeting their personal needs for time off and that sort of thing. Today they probably would say that I was a good leader, even though the leadership concept never crossed my mind. I grew up in Oklahoma where neighbors help neighbors. That's what I practiced at work and I recommend you do the same.

I learned a lot about being organized in this position because in a job that deals with numbers, things have to balance. I learned more about accounting in this job than I ever did in college. And as I said before, I had taken accounting twice in college to finally achieve a D. In business I made an A. Practical hands on experience is how I've always learned best. Don't write someone off because they don't have a certain level of formal education. *Always remember, different people learn in different ways.*

One of the first things I did in this job was to move my office next to Peter Kleiser's office in the main kitchen because, well, "He was the man."

He was the executive chef. He was the boss, and I wanted to be close to him—not only to do a good job, but also to get to know him and for him to get to know me. He would have a big say in my future. Being close to the action is one thing I learned with this move. Don't isolate yourself in a remote location. If you do, you will be forgotten and become irrelevant.

My new office was right in the middle of the kitchen with big windows overlooking the bustling kitchen action. The responsibilities of my new position were to implement strong food and beverage control systems and procedures. Being located right in the kitchen I was part of the scene, and I got to know all of the cooks, dishwashers, and other employees in the area whom I was trying to control. People knowing you and seeing you often helps a great deal in getting your work done, especially in an area like control and audit. In all future jobs in my career, I made sure my office was in the middle of the action. I'll be sure to point that out in the future positions I share about. Having comfortable relationships with people is vital for getting them to help you do your job.

Chef Kleiser taught me a lot. He was an excellent manager

and well organized. He had to have a team who could cook and serve banquets for 3,000 guests and manage several restaurants as well. He was a great leader, too. I observed how he led his team. He was a teacher, and he respected everyone at every level. He was tough but fair. He always had his meals with his team and everyone was welcome at his table no matter what position they held. I never heard him raise his voice or try to intimidate anyone as many chefs had the bad habit of doing in those days.

One time I ordered the wrong melons for a banquet for 3,000. I ordered Crenshaw melons when I was supposed to order honeydews. I will never forget what Chef Kleiser said to me. He said: "Lee, you can be a fool once or a fool all of your life. When you don't know something, *ask questions*—then you will know, and that way you will only be a fool once."

The fact is you're really only a fool if you don't know something and you fail to ask questions no one respects someone who thinks or even acts like they know everything. Being humble is a big deal and gains you a lot of credibility. So many leaders have not learned this, including me from time to time in my early career. It's usually a self-confidence and pride issue that causes us not to ask questions. I still don't do this one as well as I wish I did. My boss at Disney, Al Weiss, asked more questions than anyone I have ever known and he was never afraid to say, "I don't understand that. Please explain that to me again because I don't get it." That, I guess, is why he was the President of Disney World and later the entirety of Disney Parks and Resorts.

One of the other things I learned in the control position—which is funny now but wasn't then—is the 1,500 avocados I ordered. I didn't order them early enough, and one day out from the banquet they were still too hard to use. I ended up spreading them all over the pool deck of the hotel with blankets over them to ripen them in time for the banquet. Still to this day, I don't think I ever pick up an avocado without thinking about the importance of knowing what you're doing and the timetable you have to work with.

I think that if those avocados had not ripened, the chef would have fired me for sure—because as I recall, this was not long after the melon mishap. Can you imagine being fired over avocados? That would be a story you would not want to tell anyone or give as the reason to a future employer on why you're no longer at your last job.

I do know one thing for sure, the chef gave me lots of breaks while I learned because I had a good attitude, and I was a hard worker. That alone might be the best lesson learned for me. People can give you a break, or they can ignore you and let you fall flat on your face. A can-do attitude will often be your best attribute even if you have to fake it some days.

While I was at Disney World two college program students came to see me on the same day. The first student I saw told me that this was the worst experience of her life and a total waste of time. She continued to let me know that she had learned nothing while at the Walt Disney World® Resort in the college program. The second student came to see me later that afternoon and told me this had been the best experience of her life and that she wanted to come back after graduation. The first one actually told me that the job was beneath her. I predict, she is going to have a disappointing career. She thought that because of the college she attended she should be treated differently, but what she really needed was experience, and couldn't see that. Her self-awareness was out of focus. Frankly, nobody cares where you went to school. What they care about is what you can do and how well can you do it. The three things which will make you successful are skill, a can do attitude and passion. She had only skill. Missing two out of three is not going to serve her well.

Both of these students worked in fast food operations. I think the difference between the two was purely attitude, humility and I suspect how their parents raised them. Let me interview parents and I can pretty accurately predict what kind of employees their children will be.

I can tell you I'm as comfortable on quarry tile in a kitchen as I am on the carpet in public spaces. A lot of people are not comfortable backstage, behind the scenes because they have never experienced it. As we say in food and beverage, the kitchen is the *"Heart of the House."* The heart is a very important organ, don't you think?

Not a long time passed before I was promoted to the 2,000-room Conrad Hilton Hotel in Chicago (Chicago Hilton as it is called today) as food and beverage controller. I learned a lot of different things in this new position in Chicago. I had a larger staff, and I had food and beverage locations that were much larger, busier and more complex.

We even operated commercial production kitchens and packaging for shipment of food products to other hotels around the country. The legal and safety issues around this kind of operation are numerous, complicated, and tedious. We were shipping food across state lines, and it had to be prepared just right and inspected for all of the correct handling and packaging procedures from start to finish with numerous licensing requirements. There were many new things for me to learn and learn quickly.

The one big thing I learned in in this position was that my authority—or what I thought was my authority—would not work without good relationship skills. I dove right into the job and tried to start changing everything in the process and put new control procedures in place without establishing the right relationships with the executive chef, who'd been there long before I was born. Our relationship became so stressed that he actually banned me from the kitchen and sent me back up to my office on the executive floor to stay so as to not bother him anymore. In my previous job at the Washington Hilton, I had moved my office next to the chef so I could better my relationship with him. I forgot to do this in Chicago and paid dearly for it. I did not repeat that mistake again.

I started over the following week by apologizing to him, and it took me several months to get back to where I could start to do what I was sent there to do. I learned that you must touch the people before you touch the task. I learned that you better take the time to build trusting relationships before you try to exercise your authority.

I learned that I wasn't as big a deal as I thought I was. I knew what had to be done, but I hadn't learned that in a new environment you're going to have to start over because no one knows your capability. I was the new kid on the block and some didn't even want me there. Imagine that! I learned that when you are promoted not everyone is happy for you. I always keep track of who does and does not congratulate and encourage others when they're promoted.

Your technical and management expertise means nothing if you can't get anything done and when there's resistance, you cannot get much done. You get things done with the help of others. This is where the leadership piece comes in. If I had known back then what I know now about the importance of great leadership, I would never have fallen into the trap of arrogance. Arrogance takes you nowhere and is dangerous to both your career and those around you.

Another thing I learned was that it's important to meet in person with those you have a problem with rather than sending rude notes or emails to them. This was part of the problem I had with the chef. I would send him memos and copy his boss because I was too intimidated to go see him personally. I can tell you, this never works. I was pouring gasoline on the fire. Why had someone not taught me these things?

Experience is also a tough teacher. My boss was also intimidated by him, so I was really in a tough spot. I could not depend on my boss to get me out of this mess as he was more intimidated by the chef than I was.

One day my boss asked me, "Lee, how old are you?" I said

that I was 23 and he said, "You can't talk to people the way you do at your age." My age had nothing to do with it actually— but he was right that I could not get things done by trying to intimidate people into doing what I wanted, which was what I was doing. That was a great lesson. It is probably a fact that the younger you are, the more finesse you need to be effective, especially with older, more experienced individuals.

I did get semi-lucky though in that the chef retired shortly and a new one came and things worked well from then on. In Chapter 3 I'll tell more about salvaging my performance in Chicago. After which, I received a call to become the food and beverage controller in the most famous hotel in New York City—and maybe the most famous hotel in the world.

This hotel first stood where the Empire State Building is today and in 1929, opened on Park Avenue between 49th and 50th Streets and served more head of state office holders than any other hotel in the world. This was a whole new world for the country boy from Oklahoma! I had now earned my second million in experience, even though I couldn't afford much except the basic necessities.

I was married now, and we'd just had a baby boy, Daniel who arrived on February 18, 1969, only a few months before Neil Armstrong and Buzz Aldrin landed on the moon. With a new baby and a new job offer, life was beginning to get very adventurous!

I just found out that I was being promoted from the food and beverage controller's job at the Conrad Hilton Hotel in Chicago to The Waldorf Astoria in New York City as the food and beverage controller. This was 1969 and I was receiving a 50% increase in salary. My salary would be increasing from $8,000 a year to $12,000 a year. I was very happy because I finally thought we were in the big money and that we would be living really well. I was thinking *wow,* a 50% increase. That was huge. It turned out that 50% seemed much bigger than it actually was, especially when you're heading to NYC. The lesson here is that if things sound too good to be true, they usually are.

Things have really changed a lot today. Back in 1969, Hilton did not give you an interview trip. You just said "yes" or "no" to the offer, and if you said yes, you moved. Hilton put you up in a hotel for a few weeks while you found an apartment at your new location, and that was that. I am not sure what happened to the people who said, "No." Now, I'm pretty sure they didn't want me to get a look at the cost of housing and other expenses in New York City before I said, "Yes."

We didn't have much furniture, so it was an easy and cheap move to New York for Hilton.

The three of us arrived in New York City and reality sat in very quickly. We started looking for an apartment. This was one of those bad days I told you about earlier. We finally found an apartment we could maybe afford. It was $350 a month compared to $135 a month in Chicago. It was a small two-bedroom and had been painted about 200 times, had no air conditioning, and only had a few roaches. It was in Forest Hills, Queens at the corner of 62nd Road and 108th Street. To get to work I would have to walk a few blocks, then catch a bus to the subway station, take the subway to 53rd and Lexington, and then walk another three blocks to get to The Waldorf Astoria. My 50% increase was disappearing before my eyes. The subway was 20¢, a shoeshine was 60¢ and to get your shirts professionally cleaned and pressed was 32¢. Working at the Waldorf required crisp, white, starched, and perfectly ironed shirts.

The upside was that I had a good position in the most famous hotel in the world. I was expected to look like a million bucks and wear nice dark suits, pressed shirts, cufflinks, and polished shoes to look the part at the Waldorf. You had to look the part whether you could afford it or not.

The job turned out to have pretty much the same responsibilities as the one in Chicago, except now I was in charge of food and beverage purchasing, receiving as well as the storerooms for issuing the products not to mention I had a much larger staff to worry about. I learned a lot about food, their costs and many products that I had never even seen or heard of before. The wine and liquor selection in the Waldorf was huge.

The big thing I had learned was to get off on the right foot with the director of food and beverage and the executive chef. These two people were very powerful and if I didn't do my best, my career would be dead in the water and I wasn't about to repeat my mistakes in Chicago. *If you make a mistake, that's one thing, but if you repeat a mistake, you are a fool.*

I got off to a great start. There were a lot of control problems in the food and beverage department, so I had an opportunity to make a difference and I did a great job.

I worked hard six days a week. My day off was Thursday. I was living two lives. *I looked like a million dollars at work and was poor as a church mouse out in Queens.* This is 1969, and I have been working for almost 5 years; and I am still not making as much money as I did as a banquet server. And now I am living in the most expensive city in the United States, and I have a baby and a wife.

Our son Daniel was eating nine jars of baby food a day. I can't afford this. My shirts have to go out to the laundry. They are 32¢ a day and I can't afford this. I would leave Priscilla $6 in cash on the counter every morning. We did not have a credit card. We only spent what we could afford. Six dollars was our daily budget for everything, including the nine jars of baby food, my shirts and everything else including our food. I thought, "Why did I get into management?"

We sold our car when we moved to New York for two reasons—because we could not afford it, and because 500 cars a year were stolen in the ten square blocks where we lived in Queens, and we lived in a fairly nice neighborhood.

We definitely could not afford a garage in our neighborhood or in the city, and for sure we could not afford the high cost of car insurance.

For the next 3 years we had no car, so all of our outings on my day off were by subway or by staying close to home in the neighborhood. Without a car, Priscilla's days were busy just taking care of our family needs.

Almost every Thursday on my day off I would let Priscilla sleep late; and I would take Daniel to The Waldorf Astoria to Oscar's Restaurant for breakfast and then to Central Park. When you work six days a week and get home late, you really have to cram in that special family time.

I learned a lot about food in New York and at the Waldorf, but we could only afford cheap restaurants on my day off, if we could afford to go out at all. It seems most ethnic restaurants were pretty cheap, so those are the restaurants we ended up in. We definitely could not afford a baby sitter so Daniel went everywhere with us.

My boss at the Waldorf, Gene Scanlan, turned out to be my first real mentor. A mentor to me is someone who really wants to help you, teach you, and knows you. Mr. Scanlan as I called him sat me down day one and told me the rules for working at the greatest of them all, The Waldorf Astoria. I learned that every head of state, every queen, and every king who had ever come to New York City had stayed at The Waldorf. During meetings of the United Nations, the hotel was literally full of dignitaries, and with them, massive amounts of security.

The rules were simple:

- You work six days a week.
- Your day off will be Thursday.
- You never wear a brown suit or brown shoes after 5:00pm at The Waldorf.
- We will buy you a tuxedo, shirt, bow tie, suspenders, and cuff links.
- Anytime there is a black-tie event in the hotel, you will wear your tuxedo.

- You will not take your tuxedo home. You will keep it at work, so it is always here when you need it.

- You will need to check the events every day to make sure you are dressed properly during the day and in the evening.

- You will always look well groomed; you will always have clean, well-trimmed fingernails and polished shoes.

- You will not have tattoos or piercings that anyone can see.

- You will not have long hair, or hairstyles or colors that are not natural and professional.

- You will not look or act weird in any way. This is The Waldorf.

These were the rules and they were very clear. I learned to really enjoy clarity. If you want people to know the rules, then tell them and tell them what will happen if they don't follow them. Then, they can make the decision to work under those rules or leave. If you are in the corporate world look at the front page of the organization's annual report and see how the most successful people in your company dress. If you are in a small organization, look at the owner for clues about what works professionally. Never underestimate how much impact how you look will have on your career.

I worked as the food and beverage controller in New York for about a year, improving the controls and processes quite a lot. I had developed a good team and the day came when

I was told that I was being promoted to the position of assistant food and beverage director and would be Mr. Scanlan's assistant. This position turned out to be a lot of administrative work; working on Kosher menus for the chef and recording daily customers served and sales for the restaurants, ordering menus and supplies, and other things of that nature. This job was the stepping-stone for me to become a director of food and beverage at Hilton Hotels. Everyone in the food industry wanted this position no matter what it paid—and by the way, I received no increase in pay for this new promotion. The recession of 1970 had arrived, and we received no merit increases for 2 years.

I had basically no authority over anyone. The restaurant managers of the six restaurants knew a lot more than I did, and they pretty much only took direction from Mr. Scanlan. I learned that your title is sometimes bigger than your authority, but you probably don't want too much authority until you know what you are doing, so I was in a good place. I really liked my new business card with my name, title and the Waldorf Astoria logo in gold.

Mr. Scanlan took me under his wing and took me to every banquet and to every restaurant in the hotel, in order to teach me about the foods, beverages and the service. Every Monday night he took me and another young manager, Bill Wilkinson to dinner at 6:00pm and ordered these different foods and wines and explained to us how they were prepared, and the history of the particular dishes. This was not eating dinner, this was a class. I would never have eaten a raw oyster if Mr. Scanlan hadn't made me. I later quit eating these raw oysters and clams after Mr. Scanlan came down with hepatitis from eating them and was out of work for three months. I was sorry to see him home sick, but during this time I had the opportunity to take on a lot more responsibility, a good learning experience for me. He survived his illness and came back to work. He was healthier and I was smarter.

Mr. Scanlan took me to all of the best restaurants in New York City and involved me in special events. One night we catered a charity event at Cartier's Jewelry Store on Fifth Avenue and set up the buffets on the jewelry cases throughout the store. Outside catering is a tough business. I learned you really have to be organized. Checklists are a must and in this case, security was everywhere.

Mr. Scanlan enrolled a good friend, Dennis O'Toole, and me in the Grossman wine seminar that started at 7:30pm on Monday nights, and he paid for it in order for us to learn all about wines. I suppose this was somewhat like tuition reimbursement, which did not exist back then.

Mr. Scanlan always took a taxi home, and many nights would say, "Come on" and he would drop me at my apartment so I did not have to ride the subway home, which would have taken an hour. Instead I was home in 15 minutes by taxi. This was a big deal on a Wednesday night. I learned that these little acts of kindness are important. We should all do them when we can.

I think the thing I learned most from him was that it feels good to help others. He really liked helping others get ahead.

I could feel his generosity. To give your time to help others is a really special thing, because most of us don't have any extra time, or at least we don't think we do. If you can, be a mentor to someone. Your mentoring may make the difference for their career success. There are people all over the world today who attribute their success to Gene Scanlan who shared both his time and knowledge with them. I hope I am remembered the same way.

I remember one day he told me to order pastrami and corned beef sandwiches with cold slaw, potato salad, and pickles from six different New York delis so we could do a taste test to compare their quality with ours, to see if we could improve. I learned in this job to always look for the better way. Always focus on improvement. No decision is ever final.

Of all things, we even had a buttermilk tasting at one time. I did not like that tasting, and I still don't understand how anyone can drink it, but I have tasted buttermilk, because Mr. Scanlan made me do it. My mother could not even make me do that. That was an experience.

I remember being assigned to create a special menu for a special dinner that might have been served in the 1700s. That was the day I learned about Fiddlehead Ferns. This is not a big deal, but it does show learning never ends. He taught me how to research menu items from different eras for special events. Today with the Internet that should be much easier. Go ahead and Google Fiddlehead Fern and then you will learn something most other people don't know. You might even want to sauté some up tonight for dinner, if you can find them.

I had my first caviar and my first French champagne at The Waldorf, and I liked them both. I had my first martini in New York City, and I did not like it, but it was an experience anyway. Reading about food and beverage, and tasting it are two different things just as everything in life. Experience matters, and in my opinion, is the best teacher of all.

I received a call in my office one evening to investigate a guest complaint down in the Peacock Alley Lounge in the lobby of the Waldorf. A guest thought the cocktail server was manipulating the guest check and overcharging them. I went down, approached the waiter, and asked to see all of his guest checks. I will never forget how his hand started shaking as he took the Budweiser from his serving tray and smashed it into my right eye. Come by some day, and I will show you the six stitches.

I told my son until he was grown that I had fallen down the stairs, as I didn't want him thinking his dad was being beaten up at work. I learned to approach future investigations with more caution and to have someone else with me. I can tell you it didn't work out the way I had hoped the next time either when a few years later I was hit again and added 14 more stitches to my other eye and head by another waiter.

New York City is a rough and tough city and a very diverse place. I think one reason that I have so much appreciation and respect for diversity today is from all of those years working in the hotel business with guests and fellow employees from all over the world. If you live in places like New York City, you get exposed to so much more in the area of diversity, from food to cultures, to religions, and on and on. In New York

City, you either appreciate diversity or you don't make it. I remember what a co-worker at Disney told me one day when we were talking about diversity. He said, "In New York City I was a CPA. In Orlando I am a black CPA." In New York it is all about performance and not where you are from, what color you are or what religion you practice.

The Waldorf was a very intimidating place when I first got there, and I was really insecure. I experienced discrimination and bigotry because I was the Oklahoma college dropout country boy while most of the other managers were from the best hotel schools in the world. When I left the Waldorf for my next assignment and promotion almost 3 years later, I was very secure in my technical knowledge, my management abilities and I had learned some excellent lessons in leadership from watching Mr. Scanlan and our Executive Chef, Arno Schmidt, in action. They were intelligent, nice, respectful, competent, and tough leaders in a hotel that was known around the world for its excellence. *After having worked for 7 years, I still wasn't making the money I had hoped, but I had earned $3 million in experience.*

Priscilla, Daniel and I journey up to Tarrytown, New York, next where I am finally to be in charge something and ready to make my fourth million in experience! I did receive a salary increase for this promotion and was now up to $14,000 a year, *a thousand dollars more than I made my first year as a banquet server back in 1965, seven years earlier!*

3

MY NEXT THREE BOSSY BOSSES

1972–1973

I HAD EIGHT POSITIONS behind me now, and we have relocated from Washington, to Chicago, to New York City. As mentioned, I had been working for 7 years and once again we were relocating to Tarrytown, New York, to the Hilton Inn as the executive assistant manager and director of food and beverage. It was 1972 and I was leaving The Waldorf Astoria grandeur for a new role in a 205-room Hilton Inn. The last eight jobs and experiences I believe had prepared me well for this next promotion where I would finally oversee my own department.

I have to tell you, though, that no one up to this point had spoken to me about leadership responsibility. I have learned how to be a well-organized manager, and have improved my technical knowledge and expertise from the experiences I have had. I look back and wish my leadership behaviors had been better as I recall a couple of examples, which I will just keep to myself. I wish someone had taught me more about this area before I made some of those mistakes.

I was able to develop the *Disney Great Leader Strategies* in 1995 only after years of making mistakes and years of observing great leadership as well as poor leadership. If you want to know more about my leadership strategies read my book, *Creating Magic: 10 Common Sense Leadership Strategies from a Life at Disney,* so you too can avoid these pitfalls.

We moved out of our Queens apartment on the seventh floor that overlooked the Long Island Expressway and the 1960 World's Fair grounds. This was the noisiest apartment I ever lived in. Priscilla and I used to imagine that the sound of the traffic was the ocean. Sometimes you really need to use your imagination to survive and to go to sleep. We had made only one big purchase while living in this apartment for 3 years and that was a $35 window fan. Not air conditioning but a whole lot better than nothing.

Tarrytown, New York, on the other hand is one of the nicest, prettiest places on earth, right on the Hudson River about 40 miles north of New York City. This is also the area where Ichabod Crane and the Headless Horseman were from. I often drove over the bridge that he used to ride over to terrorize people in *The Legend of Sleepy Hollow* by Washington Irving. Back in Ichabod Crane's day, it was a wooden bridge though.

We rented a nice garden apartment on the first floor with a nice view of the woods. Lots of kids lived there, and this was really the good life after being in NY City for 3 years. The rent was even cheaper. The place was called Sleepy Hollow Apartments. Even the name was good. We of course knew the Headless Horseman hung out in Sleepy Hollow, but we didn't mention that story to Daniel. We stuck to stories from Disney and Golden Books. He was still into Mickey Mouse and Donald Duck, which were much more appropriate for him at the age of three. The Headless Horseman would have to wait until he got older. This is his third move since he was born, but at this age, kids could care less as long as mom and dad are around.

My day off was still Thursday, and we only lived about a half-mile from the hotel so the perk here was no commuting. This was a good thing since we didn't own a car. Remember, I said that *every job has good things and things that are not so good.* I have a name for this, which I'll tell you later

Within two weeks of moving to Tarrytown, I had to buy a car as we were out in the country and Priscilla couldn't go anywhere without a car. I bought an old Opal Kadette from a manager who reported to me. I paid $250 for this car, and it was on its last leg—more on this mistake later. My three million dollars worth of experience was not of much value when I needed money to buy a car, and my salary would not afford a car that was reliable.

You would think that with the great title I had now, I would be rolling in dough, but we still lived from paycheck to paycheck. Hilton did not even offer a medical plan back then. When we got sick, we paid out of our pocket. And Daniel cost us $1,200 when he was born in Chicago at the now closed Michael Reese Hospital on the South Side of Chicago and that $1,200 came right out of our pocket.

The job was good, and I found it exciting because I was in charge of something, finally. *I soon found out that being in charge brings on lots of stress coupled with long hours.* People actually expected me to make decisions and to know what I was doing. The guests too always wanted to see the person in charge, which was me, and 99% of the time they were not happy.

We performed 300+ weddings a year at the hotel. These were upscale weddings and were all attended by local people who were wealthy and demanding. They did not understand the word "No" and so I had to find alternatives that satisfied my guests. They really would not accept "No," so I had no choice but to look for clever alternatives and to improve my diplomatic and negotiation skills.

I remember one father telling me that if anything went wrong with his daughter's wedding I would be receiving lots of flowers. He was a florist. I knew what he meant and made sure I was on duty that Saturday night for his daughter's wedding. I didn't think he was joking! He meant he would be sending flowers to my funeral if his daughter did not have a perfect wedding. Sometimes excellent performance is literally a life and death scenario.

We also had the most popular restaurants in the area that

were frequented for special-occasion dining. We had to be great. We had no choice, as our guests demanded it. We had a Cabana Club, which was a club for very rich guests from New York City and Long Island who stayed with us on weekends for three months in the summer. They were rich, tough, and demanding.

I learned a lot dealing with pretty unreasonable people. I always looked after their needs and never let them see a hint of a poor attitude from me—I thought a lot of negative things, but I never expressed them to anyone. Know your role and know your part and then perform it perfectly. This is also called *professionalism.*

I worked the dining room every Friday and Saturday night, helping my restaurant manager handle special requests for guest after guest. Many times I was in the kitchen helping the executive chef plate up a banquet or even peel shrimp. Small places don't have a lot of extra help when employees call in sick.

My past experiences as a server and cook were helpful on these busy nights. I actually knew what I was doing, and the staff appreciated my help.

We knew at the Walt Disney World® Resort that one of the frontline cast member's expectations is for their leader to know their job and to be able to perform it. This is a good lesson for all of you. Can you do the work of the people you lead?

One day I even had to drive the Westchester County country roads to find a stand that sold vine-ripe beefsteak tomatoes as one of our guests was demanding them for dinner that night. I found them.

One night the kitchen was so hot that we could not get the whipping cream to thicken, and we had ruined the entire amount of whipping cream we had on hand trying to whip it. I raced off to a local restaurant to borrow two quarts of cream and then to my apartment where Priscilla whipped it up for us and I sped back to the hotel and walked right into the dining room with the bowl in my hands and served that cream right onto the fresh berries that were already in front of the guests without a moment to spare. Living close to work and having Priscilla close by to whip the cream paid off.

At the end of the dinner, the host put something in my hand and said, "Thank you, Lee, that was a great dinner." It was a dollar! I said, "Thank you!" Yes, we were allowed to take tips. He was serious. Even back then a dollar did not go far. If it had been $20, I would not have remembered it, though, and would not have a good story to tell you. Just this week, my grandson Jullian was telling me about a difficult guest who left him no tip after running up a $60 tab at the Chefs du France Restaurant at Epcot where he was a waiter this past summer. The next guest left him an $80 tip and another a $100 tip. The lesson, always take care of everyone equally and in the end it will all work out.

The days were long in Tarrytown. While managing, I went to work around 8:00am and got home between 8:00–10:00pm every evening, nearly six days a week. Over the years the more I was in charge, the longer the hours became until I took a time management seminar in 1980 and then my life changed. We will get to that story soon. Actually the guests were in charge,

I soon figured out, and this was a very good lesson. Being in charge isn't always as fun as it's cracked up to be.

I learned a lot in this role. It is different when you are the best hotel in town, especially when it is a small town. The hotel had only 205 rooms, but our food and beverage sales were more than many thousand-room hotels. Because of all of the weddings, we were one of the top hotels in the company for profit. That was a nice place to be.

In small places you get the opportunity—whether you want it or not—to do every front-line position, and you get this opportunity daily. I know what is possible. I installed home-size washers and dryers on each guest room floor, and had the housekeepers wash and dry all of the towels and washcloths every day and put them back in the guest rooms instead of sending them out to a laundry. Only the sheets went out to a commercial laundry to be processed. There are many things you learn to try, out of necessity, in small places. This also helped the bottom line immensely.

Even back then I was fascinated with motivational tapes and books on leadership and management. I bought a set of tapes on motivation and played them for thirty minutes at my weekly staff meeting, and then we would discuss them. I don't know whether my team really liked them or not, but I did and I do think they helped us gain different perspective on the subjects of management, customer service and leadership. This was a great experience. I highly value my time in Tarrytown to this day.

One good lesson I learned is that *you had better decide in advance what you stand for and know what ethical, honest leadership and behavior look like.* One day a man came to see me who owned a taxi company. He handed me an envelope and said, "All I want is for you to make sure that only my taxis are allowed to wait in front of the inn to pick up your guests." I opened the envelope and there were ten $100 bills—$1,000! I had never in my life held $1,000 in cash in my hand. I felt dizzy, and my stomach and head were spinning. Priscilla and I did not have one dime in the bank. We needed a car badly. We needed lots of things. I could think of a hundred ways to spend $1,000. If you think a thousand dollars is a lot today, just think what it was back in 1972 when you could buy a new car for $3,000. I took a deep breath and said, "Sorry. I can't do that," and handed the envelope back to him. I knew what he was asking was wrong, and I was glad that long ago I had settled my own ethical standards for honesty and integrity. Make sure you have too. It is just a matter of time until you find yourself in this position in business or in your personal life. *Know now what you stand for and what you won't stand for!*

- What would you do today if someone offered you drugs at a party?

- What would you do if you had a chance to take a little money from the register in your job and knew others were doing it?

- What would you do if your boss came to you and told you to inflate the inventory this month to make the profit look better?

- What would you do if your leader told you a way to code an invoice as expense instead of capital to slip the expense through and then told you to do it?

- What would you do if your fellow employees asked you to use your Disney Pass to help them get some of their friends or family into the parks?

- What would you do if you knew that fellow employees were abusing their discount privileges in merchandise or food?

You had better figure out right now where you stand. It's important to do the right, honest, ethical thing when you are confronted with these kinds of issues in your life. The front page of the newspaper is full of stories every single day about people who have not prepared themselves for that moment. Some go to jail, and some humiliate their families and disappoint their friends. Some commit suicide while others get divorces. There's nothing worse than having to share that aspect of truth regarding yourself or family with others.

I also had my first experience of not respecting my leader in this job. He was not making me feel special, treating me as an individual, respecting me, or making me more knowledgeable. He was a screamer, and I can't stand that. After a year of having to deal with him, I found another job in another hotel company in Dallas and quit.

The company (Hilton) went nuts and flew me to Chicago to the corporate office to meet with Porter Paris, Executive Vice President of Hilton. He put "full-court pressure" on me and talked me out of quitting. He made me feel special, and he promised me a promotion if I would stay with the company. I agreed and stayed and was soon promoted to director of food and beverage at the 1,000-room Los Angeles Hilton Hotel. I received an increase in salary to $18,000 a year. Looking back I should not have stayed at Hilton, and I'll tell you why a little later.

We now owned a good used car that was reliable. I had bought a 1972 yellow Volkswagen Bug from the general manager's secretary in Tarrytown for $2,000 in 1972. It was only a few months old. We drove that car for almost 8 years and then gave it to my brother-in-law, Hank, who drove it for two more years, and then he sold it for $400. That car ended up costing $160 a year over 10 years. That was a really good lesson in not wasting our money on cars that depreciate immediately. We still do that today. Priscilla has been driving her current car for 9 years and drove her last one for 15 years. The Opal Kadette that only ran half the time I gave away to a local sheriff who used to come to the hotel for coffee. He was going to fix it up for his son. Poor kid! You would have to be a complete idiot to leave town in this car and go out on the Interstate, so we stayed pretty close to home and always in walking distance to a car-repair center where our Opal spent most of her life.

The one perk in Tarrytown was that Priscilla and I made lifelong friends. Steve Kunis was our top catering salesman. He could even talk brides into getting married on Thursday when Saturday and Sunday were not available. Forty-four years later Steve and his wife Janice are still great friends. There is always a perk if you look for it. Great friends are much better than bad bosses.

In Tarrytown I had earned my next million, $4 million in total experience. I kept thinking, "Is all of this experience ever going to pay off in hard dollars?"

Tarrytown is where I got involved in the United Way; and I even ran the campaign back in 1972. Even back then I knew it was a good thing. I didn't do it correctly, though. I called the employees and had each one of them fill out the pledge card in front of me and sign it. We raised a lot of money, but I learned many people didn't appreciate this tactic. Live and learn! I did not repeat that tactic when I ran the United Way campaign for Disney World and for Central Florida many years later. In fact I learned a good lesson from Michael Eisner, the CEO of the Disney Company at the time. I asked him for a contribution to Orlando's United Way drive. He gave $100,000 and Roy Disney gave $50,000. I wrote Michael a thank you letter and commented that we appreciated his contribution even though it was not that much as a percentage of his wealth. One day my secretary told me that Michael Eisner was on the phone and wanted to talk to me. I was thinking no way, someone is pulling a prank. I picked up the phone and sure enough it was Michael Eisner. He said, "You made me feel bad saying my contribution was not very much. Lee you need to learn to just say thank you when someone gives you money."

He was absolutely correct. In retrospect I am thinking, what was I thinking about, was I crazy? $100,000 is a lot of money.

Our next move to Los Angles was exciting as we had never

been to California. Hilton would not transport our car, so we hired a man we did not even know to drive it to Los Angeles for us. I flew ahead to find an apartment. That yellow Volkswagen never ran the same after that 2, 800-mile drive to our new home in LA.

The downside to this move was immediate. We quickly found it was really expensive to live in California; and in those days, it was legal to deny apartments to families with children. We could not find any place near my job and ended up way out in the San Fernando Valley, from where it took me an hour to get to work; and the traffic even back then was a mess in Los Angeles. We only had one car, so Priscilla had to go to the store and other places nearby on foot or by cab in an emergency. We quickly made friends in our apartment complex with people who had two cars.

One thing was consistent, though. My day off was still Thursday. This proves that consistency is not always a good thing. Most Thursdays we would drive to Malibu or someplace like that to have lunch and let Daniel run into the freezing Pacific Ocean. He was four and when you are four, the ocean is not cold.

We did have a nice new California-style apartment, which while expensive was somewhat affordable. The place we lived in was called, "Wishing Well Apartments for Children and Their Parents." I am not kidding. If you were not fond of kids, this was not the place to live. Kids were everywhere.

I stayed in this job at the LA Hilton as food and beverage director for about a year and had another boss whom I could not get along with. I promise that it was not my fault. I really did not learn much in this role. The general manager lived in the hotel and expected me to be there day and night. He, too, was a screamer. He was technically very good, but the word leadership was not in his vocabulary or his actions.

He wouldn't have lasted a day at the Walt Disney World® Resort or at Marriott. I worked very long and hard hours in this job. This was an 8:00am–8:00pm job six days a week. You can do the math. *I did learn in this and the previous job in Tarrytown how not to be like the people I reported to.* I guess that was equivalent to some form of leadership training. One upside was making a good friend, Steve Kunis, who was a young catering manager. All these years later Steve and I and his wife Janice are still friends.

A good friend of mine, Helmut Horn, told me about a job in Lancaster, Pennsylvania, as the director of food and beverage of a privately owned hotel. The job paid 62% more than I was making in Los Angeles. I was not saving a penny in those days, was totally fed up with my pay and my boss, so I decided to check it out. The lesson here is not to make hasty decisions when you are in a poor state of mind. In the end, this one turned out all right even though the career roller coaster was running straight down in a free fall at full speed. This turned out to be a key move for me, even though it turned out different than I thought it would.

I flew out to Pennsylvania and interviewed for the job in Lancaster and came home and told Priscilla I was going to take it. It paid $30,000 a year, $12,000 more than I was making in

LA. She said she thought I was making a mistake and that I should get a contract or not go. I told her I knew what I was doing and that we were going. I figured having two bosses in a row whom I did not get along with would not get me much support for future positions at Hilton, especially since both had 20+ years with the company. I had been around only 8 years, and they were executives and I was not. My philosophy was, *"When they don't love you or you don't love them, it is time to move on."* So I divorced them. I guess you could call that a corporate divorce. The number one reason people leave a job is because they do not feel appreciated.

So off we went to Lancaster in our yellow Volkswagen. This was our fifth move, and Daniel was now 4 years old. We found a great apartment that was much cheaper than apartments in LA, and I was making a very good salary. I had finally made it. All of that experience had finally paid off. Priscilla was wrong. I told her I knew what I was doing. I am always right. It was the right move, but I was fired 90 days later with no notice and no severance pay. I have now had three bosses in a row that hadn't treated me right. All three were good managers but poor leaders, in my opinion.

I was stunned. I had worked for 90 days in a row without a day off trying to turn the place around financially. I wasn't told in the interviews that they were almost bankrupt or on a cash-only basis for purchases. *So much for taking a job for the money.* Be careful in your future interviews. While I was at Disney World I would get calls from former cast members wanting to return to the Walt Disney World® Resort who were misled with all of the promises from the company they had joined. The grass often turns out to be brown and not the promised green. *The grass is definitely not always greener.* That is a really good thing to remember. If you think things are bad where you are right now in your career, read on!

I was called in and told, "You have not made progress fast enough. You are fired." This all took place in less than two minutes. At 5:02pm I was unemployed in Lancaster, Pennsylvania. Okay, so Priscilla was right. Okay, so I am not always right. I went home and said, "Priscilla, I was fired today." She said without hesitation, "Good. I don't like it here anyway." There were many other things she could have said.

I married a saint. She never once said, "I told you so. I told you to get a contract. I told you that you were making a mistake." She never once said that. This was a great lesson for me, and one you should pay attention to. She may have thought it, but she did not say it. She has always stood by me for these last 48 years and I have done a lot of stupid things ... well, a couple at least. Priscilla did have great role models growing up. Her dad, Charlie, was an officer in the Navy and her mother an English teacher. They had moved twelve times before she met me; so this had been her seventeenth move. Her dad ended up becoming a rear admiral, so at least the moves paid off for their family, as they eventually would for ours.

I am now 28 years old with a wife, a four-year-old son, car payments and I have 8 years of quality experience, but I burnt my bridges at Hilton and have no job and no savings. *The lesson here is don't burn your bridges.* Leave professionally and just tell them you hate to leave. Telling your boss that you think he's a jerk and a poor example of a leader may not be the best strategy, especially if you want to come back or receive a reference from them someday. *The other lesson, try to save a few dollars a month just in case of an emergency.*

We called United Van Lines and told them to pick up our furniture and to put it into storage as we were hitting the road to look for a job. They came one day later and picked up everything we owned, except the car and our packed suitcases. It didn't take them long to pack up, as we did not own much.

The apartment complex we were living in promptly slapped a lien on our furniture because we were moving out and breaking a two-year lease after only 90 days. The sheriff confiscated everything, and we could not get it back until we paid $2,000 to the apartment leasing company. This was not a good day.

Luckily I had bought a whole-life insurance policy 8 years before at my first job and paid monthly payments on it. It had accumulated a $2,000 cash value. I sold the policy, got the lien removed, and then we headed off down the road in our yellow VW Bug to look for a job. Now even my back-up whole-life insurance cash-value policy is gone. Things are not looking good. This is definitely a personal recession heading toward a depression if I didn't find a job quickly.

I learned a lot more in this experience than I wanted to, as you can imagine. First, I didn't think it was possible for me to get fired. At the time it was the worst thing that had ever happened to me in my entire life, except when a senior girl in high school wouldn't go out with me because I was a junior and Priscilla not wanting to go out to lunch or dinner with me back in 1966 because she said that I had a bad attitude. Looking back I can see how she might have gotten that impression. A year later she agreed to go to lunch with me, and the rest is history. The upside was that getting fired eventually got me to a better place. It's funny how things work out sometimes. I found out there is life after being fired. Second, I never imagined people could be so tough. Third, I never thought about the legal ramifications of breaking a lease. I probably did not even read the lease before signing it. I do now. I quickly learned that when you are unemployed, most people who you thought were your friends and former associates don't call you back and don't help you like you hoped they would.

I learned that who you thought were your friends aren't always your friends, and other friends become extra special in a time like this and really come through for you. Remember that saying, "A friend in need is a friend indeed." We were in a big need back in 1973 like many people are today. Today I go out of my way to help my friends and family when they really need me, no matter what they need.

Let me tell you, I was in need. First, we drove to see our friends, Suzie and Alain Piallat in New York. (They put us up and fed us). I worked the phones every day looking for a job. Then we drove to Priscilla's parents in Mississippi who put us up. Thank God for family and real friends. My father-in-law, Admiral Payne, took me out to lunch to give me some coaching and counseling on how to change jobs in a more organized and secure way. He already intimidated me, even before this lunch. It took me 15 years before I could call him Charlie. That was a long lunch but a good lesson. I will never forget that crab sandwich I ordered and never ate that day. I just kind of lost my appetite as he was coaching me.

I always joked with him after that, that I thought he was afraid we were going to move in with him and Sunshine—and he would have an unemployed son-in-law for the rest of his life lying on the couch watching television. I did not tell him this joke until years later. At the time though it wasn't funny. It in fact seemed possible. He was proud of me and told me so when he and Sunshine came to visit us in Paris just a few months before his death in 1993.

I got up every morning and worked the phones. I finally made contact with someone I knew from my old days at Hilton in Chicago, Bud Davis. We did not know each other personally, but we both knew about each other. I knew he was great, and he told me that he had heard that I was. *My good performance at Hilton paid off.* Bud had moved to Marriott, this little unheard of hotel/motel company in 1973 with 32 hotels. My hotel friends all told me not to join this little unknown company, as it would never be anything. Boy, were they wrong. So much for their advice!

So in these last three jobs, I had really earned a lot in experience. The value of my experience was now up to the $4 million I projected, but I still had no real income and no savings. I do have my family, though. If you think tough times are tough, I can't even imagine how I would have gotten through this without my family being there for me and having faith in my ability. This was 1973, and the United States was about to go into a two-year recession, lasting until 1975. This was not a good time to be looking for a job. I was having my own personal depression economically and mentally without the United States having one too.

Years later my mother-in-law, Sunshine, needle-pointed a pillow for me that said, *"Behind Every Successful Man Stands a Surprised Mother-In-Law."* She did ask Priscilla if it was okay to give it to me. She is nice! I always wondered if getting fired gave her the idea for that pillow. She also told me that if I had not married Priscilla, she would have adopted me. Now that is pretty cool. Later on I put a brass plaque on a bedroom suite we have in our home that read, "Sunshine Suite." She loved that.

In the next chapter I will tell you about the rebuilding process related to careers when things don't go quite the way you had planned or hoped they would. *Things that go up might come down, but they can go back up if you stay focused, positive, and learn from your mistakes*—plus look at all of the great stories I have now.

4

STARTING OVER

1973–1979

I<small>T'S</small> **1973** and here I was still unemployed, living with my mother and father-in-law after being fired, but I was finally able to get in touch with someone from my old Hilton days who knew of me. His name was Bud David. He had moved from Hilton to Marriott as vice president of food and beverage. I called him, and he had me drive to Marriott headquarters on River Road in Washington, D.C., for an interview. I had the interview with Bud and some other executives and then took a leadership and management profile test called the Wittrick. This test was physiological to determine if I would fit well with the Marriott.

I Googled the "Wittrick Test" today as I am writing this

chapter and found out that it no longer exists, but there are plenty of others out there that you will probably run into as you apply for positions. Organizations today not only want to know what you know, but how you think, how disciplined you are, what kind of judgment you have, how much empathy for others you have, your relationship abilities with others and so forth. They want to know not only what you can do but also how you will do it.

The one thing my Wittrick Test pointed out that probably wasn't the best thing was that I had some problems with authority. It turns out that is true. I am not too fond of people telling me what to do and using their authority to push me around. I have seen many people abusing their authority in all walks of life from parents, to bosses to law enforcement. This has gotten me into a few problems from time to time in my career. That's probably why I have quit two jobs and had a few run-ins with some of my bosses over the years. I don't have a problem when I have a boss whom I respect and one that sets a good example, respects my opinion, and involves me in decisions affecting my work, but I don't work well or react well to people who can only get results through using their authority. This is the classic behavior of bullies. I have a basic distrust of people in positions of authority. Maybe I need to get counseling to overcome this problem. At 72 it might be a bit late even though a favorite quote of mine is, "It is never too late to get better."

I guess I passed the test because Bud called me and said, "Lee, we have the perfect job for you in Philadelphia as a manager." The title was complex manager for two restaurants. The first was for a lounge and room service and the second, a recreation, food and beverage area. It paid exactly what I was making back in Los Angeles a few months ago. *The lesson here: to make more money, you have to stay employed where you are being paid the higher salary.* Remember, I had a higher salary in Lancaster, but I was fired after 90 days, so my annual salary for all of 1973 was lower than what I made before I left the Los Angles Hilton.

There was one fabulous benefit, which I did not understand at the time. Marriott awarded stock options to positions even at my level as a complex restaurant manager.

I threw them in a drawer at home and forgot about them, as I had no idea what a stock option was. It turned out that these stock options had huge value a few years later and in fact paid for Daniel to go to Boston University for 4 years and for Priscilla to get a really nice diamond ring since we could finally afford it after all of these years of being married. So all in all my income went up dramatically even if I did not understand it at the time. I was just happy to be employed again.

When I heard the title of "complex manager," I wondered if that was the required personality or the real title of the position. I think it is best to label positions that can be identified with what the responsibilities are. I am sure that not one guest understood that title on my nametag. I told Priscilla the job was potentially in Philadelphia. She said in an alarmed voice, "Philadelphia!" We had never been there, and for some reason we had a negative opinion of Philadelphia. I guess we had watched too much television. It turned out to be one of the best places we ever lived. As they say, "Home is where the heart is." And your heart is usually where your family is.

I drove to Philadelphia and had my second round of interviews with the General Manager, Dick Stormont, and the director of food and beverage. I found out later that after my interview they both had recommended to Bud Davis not to hire me as I was too quiet in the interview and did not show much enthusiasm. They said I was "too low key." Actually, believe it or not, that was my nickname at Marriott for several years, "Low-Key Lee."

My philosophy in those days, and frankly my introverted personality, was to let my résumé speak for itself. I really did not know how to sell myself. I don't do that anymore. Today I have learned to tell people:

- What I can do for them in great detail
- What my strengths are
- What they can expect from me
- What are my weaknesses

I was a real introvert early in my career and terrified of public speaking. I just quietly did my job. I will tell you in a later chapter the downside of being poor at public speaking when you are in a leadership position and how being, too low key can be misunderstood, but you don't want to be a bragging loudmouth either.

I am a closet introvert, but have had to learn how to act like an extrovert. This can be done, I have learned, through courses, reading, and practicing. The main reason I am more of an extrovert now is that my self-confidence and self-esteem have improved as I have had more and more successes in my life.

One thing to remember is that if you are not good at something and that thing is important to your future, then it's simply something that needs to be worked on before it hurts you or hurts your career.

You probably already know what you need to work on so don't be afraid to ask someone who you know will be truthful with you and encourage you in the process.

Being able to communicate and speak in public is important in any leadership position. Leaders spend a lot of time influencing others through communication and personal example. If you're unable to speak with others about what you believe in and what you want them to do, you are going to have limited success in leading others to the results you are trying to achieve. Most people are more afraid of public speaking than they are of death. Death cannot be avoided, but being a poor communicator can. We'll talk more about that a little later though.

Well I got lucky and Bud Davis exercised his authority and told them to hire me. I didn't know this until years later, or I would probably have been even more insecure than I already was. I must admit I had to eat some humble pie. This new position wasn't the same director of food and beverage position that I had already worked at earlier in my career at Hilton. It also takes quite a lot of arrogance out of you when you get fired. I had to take it down a notch; I'll tell you that *eating humble pie is better than not eating at all—and it turned out to be the best thing that ever happened to me.* By taking this position, I gained a lot of experience that I really needed and had not had the opportunity to gain in the past. This experience would serve me well in the future.

Before I could report to my new position in Philadelphia, I was sent to the Boston Marriott for a month of training. This was the benchmark hotel in food and beverage systems and food quality at the time for Marriott. Relocation policies back then were not what they are today. Priscilla and I were expected to find our own accommodations and to pay for them personally during this month-long training period. This we quickly found out was impossible.

I called and told my hard luck story to Bud Davis. He made an exception to the policy and put us up in the hotel. My meals would be covered but not Priscilla's and Daniels. Relocation policies have come a long way since those days. We were so poor that we would order a cheeseburger platter and share it. I know you might find that hard to believe, but it's the truth.

Up to this time, this was turning out to be the worst year of my life but it would all turn out okay eventually. 1973 was a key year in my career. It was a rebuilding year of sorts and I learned many lessons that year that I wouldn't soon forget when faced with future decisions.

The training in Boston turned out to be great and I learned a lot. The Director of Food and Beverage, Olaf Arnheim, took a personal interest in my training there. He had been with the Marriott since leaving college and was a real expert in the food and beverage business. I was lucky to train under him. He had especially strong management skills and was very organized as well as very, very candid. You always knew where you stood with Olaf. He was a great coach for me. He was a leader I respected, so it did not bother me when he was brutally candid with me.

I finished my training, and the three of us headed to Philadelphia in our yellow Volkswagen Bug to report to the new job. We found an apartment in Phoenixville, Pennsylvania, that we could afford nine days before Christmas 1973.

This was a good Christmas since I finally had a job. Thank you, Santa! I promise to be good this year was all I could think of! I was so glad that 1973 was about to end. I made several New Year's Resolutions on New Year's Eve.

One of the great perks in this new job was that it was a five day workweek. The expectation for management at Marriott was five days and a 10-hour day. It seemed like doing it in 10 hours a day was harder in food and beverage than any other department but having two days off was fabulous. It is interesting what can make you happy in life.

I was sure that I was going to have Thursday withdrawal as I moved to Sunday and Monday off after working for 8 years, six days a week, and every holiday at Hilton. Priscilla and I had never spent a New Year's Eve together, or any other holiday for that matter, since we had gotten married 5 years earlier.

Priscilla became the neighborhood babysitter wherever we lived. I think some people thought she was divorced, as I wasn't around much the first few years.

Food and beverage professionals miss a lot of neighborhood parties and are always late to family gatherings. Actually, I lost track of the time between the time Daniel started to walk and when he started to talk. That I regret, but he turned out all right thanks to his mother being there and keeping an eagle eye on him. I have made up for this by spending lots of time with my grandchildren Jullian, Margot and Tristan.

My new position turned out to be a great experience, as I had never managed a group of restaurants like this. These restaurants were very busy, and the service standards were very high at Marriott. These were the days of the salad bar and lobster or prime rib dinners for $5.95. The 1973–1975 recession triggered these new high-value, complete-dinner concepts to try to drive business into hotel restaurants. Almost every restaurant had a salad bar in those days. These concepts also reduced labor cost because of the simpler food production with a narrower menu selection.

Many good ideas are born out of recessions, I have learned. You learn to try lots of things. Recessions are great at breaking down resistance to change. If you are resistant to change in a recession or business downturn, you are usually not employed by the time the recession ends. Great leaders support and drive continuous improvement through their own personal example and often have to push through the resistance that they encounter. They often stand alone when quick and decisive change must happen. That is why they say, *"It is lonely at the top." There are only two reasons people change, education or crisis.*

I was also in charge of the kitchen, and the chef reported

to me. She was a lady who had been with the company for 40 years. I did not order her around. Her nickname with the employees was "Mom." Her real name was Helen Malishka. You don't order people around when they're called Mom, especially when they know a lot more than you do, and they know that they know more than you do. She took me under her wing and taught me so much about food production, sanitation, proper storage, dating, rotation of food, proper cooking methods, and safety both in food handling and work habits. Remember that you can develop your boss if you do it with finesse. Mom did a great job in training and developing me.

The one thing that still stays with me was the concept at Marriott called, *"Clean As You Go!"* This basically meant that everyone kept the place clean. If you were a cook and dropped an eggshell, you picked it up. The kitchens and the kitchen floors were spotless and always kept dry. Accident frequency was half of what every other hotel company ran. We could all learn from this sort of simple but clear rule. The employees met this expectation because there were consequences for not keeping the place spotless and safe. *Be clear with your employees and they will deliver for you.*

In this position I learned to have strong processes and checklists in place and make sure that no one went home at the end of their shift before their work was completed. Back then, as today we would have visits from executives from time to time including Bill Marriott, the CEO of the company.

Everyone would run around saying that we had to get ready for these VIPs. I made a policy of never saying or doing this. I made sure that our areas always looked good and that we were ready at any time for anyone. I just did not like the concept of getting ready for someone. This seemed to me to be very manipulative and semi-dishonest. I heard often during my time at the Walt Disney World® Resort about managers who would tell their fellow cast members to get ready for someone, like Michael Eisner, Bob Iger, Al Weiss, and even little old me. What they were really saying was to cover up and make things look better than they usually are. I just made sure that one of my managers or I checked out all of our employees before they went home to make sure they had completed their work properly and then, we were always ready!

I heard once that when I was first in charge of the park operations at Walt Disney World and visited one of the attractions at Epcot, the manager on duty was afraid that it looked as though they were overstaffed, so the manager quickly asked some of the cast members to stay in a closet until I left. Isn't that the most bizarre and silly thing you ever heard? This may be an urban legend, but I have heard it many times over the years. I hope it is not true.

At one point-long before electronic clocking in/out was invented, I carried the timecards in my back pocket and when our employees wanted a break, they came to me, when they returned from break, they gave me their card back, and when they were ready to go home, they came to say good-bye. Before I would let them leave I would check out their work area and then give them their timecard so they could clock out. No one was able to slip out without doing his or her work; therefore, we were always ready and eventually I did not have to check their work any longer or hold onto their time cards because they knew what I expected and they met the expectations knowing I would check. Another perk in this position was that it was a bonus position. A big factor in my bonus calculation was based on accident frequency. This got myself and everyone focused on safety. More about this a little later.

Expectations and consequences are some of the important lessons I learned in this role. *The only way to have quality in anything is through education and enforcement.* This was the big lesson I learned at the Philadelphia Marriott. And one that Bill Marriott personally told me. He said, "Lee, the only way you get excellence in any organization is through education and enforcement." Most leaders do okay with the education (training) part but fall flat on their faces when it comes to enforcement (discipline).

At this job I was taught how to coach and counsel employees. There was extensive training on this subject. There was no union, but we had what was called the "Fair Treatment" policy. It was leadership's responsibility to coach, counsel, and discipline employees. The coaching had to be documented and put in writing. If the employee felt he or she was being treated unfairly, the employee could go to the next level and all the way up to the president of the company, Mr. Marriott himself.

Being able to coach and counsel people were wonderful things to learn because it's for their benefit. Doing the coaching, counseling, and discipline right away when the employee has just done something right or wrong was one of the greatest lessons of my life. Part of good coaching is giving employees any appreciation, recognition and encouragement they deserve. Remember that the number one reason employees leave a company is they do not feel appreciated.

I admired "Chef Mom" a lot. I was the boss, and she was Mom. I listened to her and learned from her, and we became great partners. I learned there that the title "boss" is not a great title unless you like being bossy.

Today I think that most people would tell you that I don't order them around. I work with my team to arrive at the best solutions. I don't make people do many things. I do, though, use every ounce of my experience, teaching, persuasion abilities, and any other talent I have to make my point of view understood; and then I listen to their point of view until we arrive at the right place. Don't fall madly in love with your idea until you have heard from others. Stay open-minded and flexible. I learned this working with Mom. We need fewer bosses and more teachers in the world.

At one point after about three weeks in this position, I had not seen or heard from the general manager or the food and beverage director and I was dealing with some very tough issues. The place was a mess. I told Priscilla one night, "I think I made the biggest mistake of my life taking this job." I was getting no feedback on my performance and remember, I am a "recovering fired person," so I was very insecure. The very next day, I opened my mail and there was a note from the general manager that read:

Dear Lee,
I am sorry that I have not seen you since you started. I have
been tied up in Washington working on some new projects.
I just want to tell you that I am hearing great things from
everyone about what a great job you are doing. We are really
happy to have you on our team. You are making a difference.
Sincerely, Richard

That day, I learned how important timely recognition is. This one note boosted my performance and my self-confidence, which is one thing you need to do your best work. Don't ever forget this lesson in all parts of your life. I still have that note. Building self-esteem and self-confidence is one of the things great leaders do. Giving people positive feedback is the fuel that drives performance. This fuel is more powerful than the solid, rocket-booster fuel that was used to launch the space shuttles, and it's free, in great supply, and in great demand. What a great fuel! I figured if I needed it so badly, others must as well. Fuel your team often so they can soar in their performance. In my first book, *Creating Magic*, Strategy 7 is titled, "Burn the Free Fuel." That fuel I named A.R.E. for Appreciation, Recognition and Encouragement. This fuel changes lives, improves performance and enhances the bottom line.

I worked in this position for about a year, and was then promoted to the position of director of restaurants. This was a larger job in another part of the hotel. It included being responsible for a high-volume, 24-hour coffee shop, The Fairfield Inn, a specialty restaurant steakhouse, the Sirloin and Saddle, a large live-entertainment lounge, the Windjammer Lounge and a smaller lounge. I had responsibility for all food and beverage purchasing and controls. I used all of my prior experience to put in place well-organized system and processes for running this operation. I focused on putting in the right processes, operating guidelines, checklists and controls. In food and beverage, tight controls are vital if you are to be profitable as the margins in this business are already challenging. Profits can literally be eaten up by employees unless you have effective policies and systems and you enforce them.

I focused heavily on training. I insisted the managers always be on the restaurant floor and available to staff for any problems they had. I set a good example for everyone by being out there in the operation myself when it was busy, bussing tables, seating guests, and even washing dishes and mopping floors. I had *learned the value of leading from the front lines and not from the office.*

I taught the managers how to do proper shift turnovers with an hour overlap so that everything was in order for the shift that was about to begin. I put a policy in place that the manager going off duty could not leave until the manager coming on duty was happy with the way the place looked and the way it was stocked. Shift-ending time for management was when all of their responsibilities were completed rather than a set time like four or five o'clock.

I put in place a monthly Saturday morning meeting for two hours, and every manager was required to be there, whether it was his or her sixth day or not. With a 24-hour operation and days off, the entire team would never have been together to work out operational issues and to agree on consistent guidelines without this meeting.

We used a checklist for everything. This was a 24-hour restaurant that served nearly 4,000 guests a day. Being organized with staffing, equipment, and food production was critical. This job taught me a lot about how to organize for high volume and the importance of consistent guidelines for all employees. *I still to this day believe that a basic checklist on a clipboard is one of the most effective tools there is for keeping a business under control.* Technology and computers are nice, but a good old clipboard and checklist are still my best friends. They never crash or need charging and everyone can afford one.

All in all, I did a very good job here. The one thing that I thought I had learned was how to coach and counsel employees about performance and behaviors. I was about to learn that this was not yet one of my top skills though.

I had a long-time waiter who caused a lot of disruption with everyone else in the organization. He was a real problem. I had spoken to him before, but it was always his word against the other person's. He was very clever in not having any witnesses around when he said very inappropriate things to other employees just to get a reaction from them and to cause trouble.

One day he made a very disparaging remark to a Japanese cashier about her culture. She reported this to me and was crying. Once again there were no witnesses, but I was fed up at this point, so I called him into my office. This time I did not do it alone.

I had his manager come into the office too, just in case. I was still remembering that time in New York when the waiter hit me with the Budweiser bottle when I was alone. You don't forget those things.

We sat down in my office, and I reviewed with him the history of the complaints I had received about him from his fellow workers as I had done with him before. He just flatly denied that he had ever done anything and told me to prove it or shut up. I then made the mistake of putting my index finger about one inch from his nose saying, "Mr. Roberts, you have a bad attitude." He immediately reacted in a rage and knocked me out of my chair; his manager and I ran out of the office toward the cocktail lounge to get away from him, he hit me over the head with a clipboard that was hanging on the wall. This is the downside of having checklist clipboards hanging in your office. Now I have 14 more stitches, not counting the six I got in New York City. I was right. He had a bad attitude. Being right is not always important though, especially when you are bleeding from several places on your head.

Priscilla said that night, "Lee, do you think this happens because of the way you talk to people?" She may have been right and it has never happened again since 1975. I learned never to stick my finger in someone's face again and announce my opinion of that person in such a straightforward, aggressive manner. I guess I am a slow learner on some things.

Well by now we were in the middle of a major recession. We let ten percent of the employees, including management go. This was the first recession that had affected me like this.

The one in 1970 included not receiving a merit increase, but I had never had to do mass layoffs before.

Before that time I didn't even know what a recession really was. This was the recession where you had to wait two hours in line to get gas because of the fuel shortage. Having to lay off so many employees was a very difficult thing for me to go through. Putting people out of work during a time when you know they won't be able to find a job is extremely tough. I quickly learned that a recession is when your sales are going down, and you need to shed costs fast. Orders from headquarters came in, and we had to implement those orders immediately.

The new general manager arrived and lucky for me it was Bud Davis who had been instrumental in hiring me just 2 years earlier. This was good for me. The only thing you can do, is reduce costs as much as possible while attempting not to hurt your brand. Shortly after Bud's arrival, my boss, Hubert Roetherdt, Director of Food and Beverage, retired.

I was sure that I would get the job. I was ready. I had the right experience; and my performance was highly rated. I had been a director of food and beverage before. There was no way that I would not get the promotion to director of food and beverage. I was already thinking of how I would spend the extra money. I had already told Priscilla that I was going to get this promotion. I think she had told her mom and dad. The recession was going to affect me too, I soon found out.

Olaf Arnheim, the man who had trained me in Boston when I started with Marriott 2 years before, had moved on to a resident manager position at the Boston Marriott, which was the job previous to becoming a general manager in those days. Because of the recession, these resident manager positions were eliminated in the entire company, and the resident managers were redeployed.

It was announced that Olaf would be our new food and beverage director. I was really disappointed. First fired, and now passed over. I am not enjoying this. I was not feeling special or respected. I came to work on Monday morning, and Olaf was standing at the back dock door where the employee entrance was as this was also the security checkpoint. No employee was allowed to enter or exit the hotel any other way.

Olaf said, "Hi, Lee. I have two questions for you. First, how do you feel about me getting the job instead of you? Second, do you think you are making the right salary for your current responsibilities?"

Wow! Did that catch me off guard! I said, "I am okay with you getting the job; and yes, I am paid properly." From that one experience I learned immediately to deal with things that people are already thinking and put them to rest so you can get on with the work. I love people who are candid and straight-forward. I learned how to do this from Olaf. A year later Olaf was promoted to be the general manager of a Marriott hotel in Saddlebrook, New Jersey.

This time I was sure I would be promoted to director of food and beverage. After all, I had been a good soldier. I had supported Olaf. I had kept a good attitude. I had been his right arm. I had achieved great business results. I had displayed patience. I thought he trusted me, and now he and Bud would decide who would get the job.

I GOT THE JOB!!!!

There are many lessons to be learned from this experience. One is that *success is a journey and not a destination.* This additional year as the restaurant manager really was a drop in the ocean looking back. It really did not affect my career at all, even though back then I thought it was the end of the world. Patience really is a virtue. My positive attitude and support of Olaf is why he selected me to take his place. He trusted me, and that's why he recommended me to Bud as his replacement.

Another year passes, and I get a call from Bud. He tells me that he is leaving to be the opening general manager of the new Marriott on Michigan Avenue in Chicago, and Olaf is coming back to Philadelphia as the general manager. That sounded great to me because I had a lot of respect for Olaf and was glad he would be my new boss.

Bud taught me a lot before he left. The one big thing he helped me with was how to be *less defensive.* In those days when I received some negative feedback on anything to do with my responsibilities, I would immediately go into battle stations and become defensive. I'd give a million reasons why that particular thing was wrong or misunderstood. I took everything personally.

Bud told me that my eyes would turn red, and I would get pale, turn white, and just focus on defending myself. He would stop me, and coach me, and make me see how foolish I was being, plus he helped me understand how this kind of behavior would hurt my career going forward. I remember one day he called me and said that he received a complaint from a regular guest that her tea was often cold. I immediately started to tell him all of the excuses why this could not be possible in *my* restaurant. He stopped me and said, "First of all, it is not your restaurant; and Lee, we are talking about cold tea. This is about the tea and not about Lee. The whole world is not about Lee. Go check to see if the cups and the water are hot."

Thank you, Bud Davis, for helping me with this behavioral problem. Today I just hate dealing with defensive people. I'm still working on that insecurity. *Being defensive at home or at work is not a good thing.* It may be the biggest reason why some people don't get candid feedback from others. When you get out of control and overreact, people just quit communicating with you. Priscilla says I still have a ways to go in this area at home. I have learned that repeating the phrase, *"Let It Go,"* over and over helps me react better when I am getting feedback I don't like. Great lesson here! If you have this issue, just let it go just like Elsa did in *Frozen*. She was the queen but still had to learn not to abuse her position and powers. My advice is, *Let It Go, Let It Go, Let it Go!*

Another thing that Bud helped me with was pricing. I remember the day we raised coffee from 30¢ a cup to 35¢ and a hamburger platter from $1.95 to $2.05. I could not imagine how we could go over the $2 mark for a hamburger platter. I was sure that all of our local guests would never come back. I fought the price increase tooth and nail.

Bud said, "Lee, if you have great coffee and a great burger

with hot, crispy French fries and fresh tomato, lettuce, and center-cut red onion with a nice big dill pickle—and you butter and grill the bun and salt and pepper the fresh meat—*quality will win out.*" He was right. Our guest counts continued to increase and not decrease as I had worried about. If you are famous for quality, then focus on quality was a great lesson I learned working for Bud. Disney, Hilton and Marriott have always known that quality will win out. It's not about the price; it's about the value. Was it worth the price I paid? These three companies have been around a long time and are going strong. When you think of their brand, you think of quality. Price is what you pay. Value is what you get.

The U.S. recession had ended, but soon the city of Philadelphia had its own personal recession in 1976. This should have been a great year for business for Philadelphia as this was the bicentennial year of the signing of the Declaration of Independence. Remember, 200 years before in Philadelphia our forefathers had signed the Declaration of Independence on July 4, 1776. This would have been a really big year for visitors and all of the hotels would have been full, that is until several people staying in a hotel in downtown Philadelphia died suddenly.

They were diagnosed with a new disease caused by a fungus build-up in air-conditioning systems. The disease was named Legionnaire's disease because the hotel guests were attending an American Legion Convention. The room cancellations began immediately after these people died, and Philadelphia found itself in its own little recession as visitors cancelled their hotel reservations in large numbers.

Here we went again looking for ways to save, reducing expenses and implementing layoffs.

I had worked for Olaf for just a few months when he called me over to his office to tell me that Bud wanted to talk to me about being the opening director of food and beverage at the Chicago Marriott. This Bud/Olaf thing was working out pretty well for me. This would be the biggest food and beverage operation for Marriott at the time—I could not believe it. All was going well. I was on a roll. Someone loved me again. Life was looking up. Being fired was becoming a distant memory. I am up to 80 percent in self-confidence, and my self-esteem is healthy. I knew that I was getting this job because both Olaf and Bud had talked and agreed that I had both the talent and experience to do it.

Careers can be like roller coasters. When they are going up, things are pretty smooth, fun, and calm—and when they go down, life is scary. Most roller coasters go up again after a fall, and you can too. The difference between success and disappointment after a career stumble is usually the attitude you display and the tenacity you have to hang in there.

I talked to Bud on the phone. He knew me, and I knew him so I didn't have to go for an interview. Priscilla and I flew to Chicago on a Friday. We bought a house on Saturday. We went home on Sunday, packed, and moved. Never buy a house that quickly.

This is our eighth move. It is 1977. Daniel is nine. I have now been working for almost 13 years. We had bought our first house in Berwyn, Pennsylvania, a suburb of Philadelphia.

It was a small house. With repairs and having to sell it only 2 years later to make the move to Chicago, we lost money. The only reason we could buy it in the first place was because my mother was willing to lend us the down payment, which I eventually repaid many, many years later. We also now have two Volkswagens. Priscilla's dad bought a house in New York, and the owners left a white Volkswagen in the garage. He gave it to us. We were now a two-VW Bug family. That white one died after about a year, and we bought a third one from one of my managers, Steve Bradley, who was being transferred to the Barbados Marriott. He gave us a really good price on it because the *Philadelphia Inquirer* newspaper was on strike and wasn't able to get an ad in the classifieds to sell it.

We bought a more expensive house in Chicago and lost money on it too when we moved again 2 years later. All of the people I knew said they were making tons of money when they sold a house. It never happened to us. Looking back I wish we had just rented for a little while longer.

The job at the Chicago Marriott was great. It was exciting to be doing all of the planning, hiring all of the managers, and working like a farm dog. The first six months were great as we were in pre-opening. The hard work started when we opened. We opened with the National Restaurant Association Convention. Every guest room, every restaurant, and every banquet room was full. This was the hardest job of my life as of 1978.

Where did that five-day workweek go?

On opening day, J.W. Marriott Sr., the chairman and founder of the company, his wife Alice, the co-founder, and their son J. W. (Bill) Marriott Jr., the President and CEO, and his wife Donna asked me to sit down and have breakfast with them. The name of the restaurant was Allie's Bakery, named after Mrs. Marriott (Alice). This is the last place I wanted to be on opening day.

I had just ordered a cup of coffee and as the server was bringing the cream, he stumbled and spilled the whole pitcher on Bill Marriott's brand new tan suede jacket. In that half-second, I saw my life flash before my eyes. I saw the light. I was dead. Bill was very nice about it and said something like, "Those kinds of things always happen to me. I think I make people nervous." That was the understatement of the day as far as I was concerned. Bill did put me at ease—another sign of a great leader. I was back, I had seen the light … and I was back. My life had been spared. *Whew.*

While waiting for our food to arrive, I was being lectured by Mrs. Marriott (Alice) on how to make a proper chili. She was telling me that you always use pinto beans and never kidney beans. About that time their food came; after a few minutes and a few bites of her breakfast, Mrs. Marriott turned to me and said, "Lee, if you don't fix the food in here I am going to take my name off of this restaurant." I saw the light again. I am dead for sure. I said, "Yes, Mrs. Marriott, don't worry I will take care of it." She said, "Okay Lee, you do that. I know that opening day is difficult, but I want you to make this place great." Once again I experienced clarity with understanding. She was clear and I understood what she wanted me to do. That is real communication. There was no misunderstanding on my part or her part. Ask yourself if you communicate with clarity, leaving no room for misunderstandings. This one thing will improve your performance and the performance of your team dramatically. Have the courage to tell the truth!

I was back for the second time … I was given understanding. I was alive. I had not been defensive, and it had worked. I excused myself and went to have a heart-to-heart talk with my chef. You don't know what pressure is until you have had a day like this—and an opening day with the Marriott family to boot.

It was clear to me very quickly which leaders were competent and which ones were not. Everyone seems to be competent in pre-opening. When guests show up, its show time and you find out quickly what everyone is made of.

I had never fired a manager in my life for performance, but I had to in this job. The first one was someone whom I had worked with before and whom I had recruited and talked into coming to Chicago, leaving his old company. It turned out that he just couldn't get the place organized. His department was a mess, and he was in a key position. I put it off for too long, and one day Bud told me he was going to fire me if I did not act. It was one of the hardest things I had had to do up to that point in my career.

A few years later in the time management seminar I took, the instructor said one thing that put leadership into perspective. He said, *"A leader's job is to do what has to be done, when it has to be done, in the way it should be done, whether you like it or not."* I love that phrase and have never forgotten it. I wish I had taken that course earlier in my career. Even today I think about that statement when I have something difficult that I have to do. This statement helped us in raising our son Daniel as well.

In those days I would beat around the bush and tell the person at the end of an hour conversation that I had to let him or her go. I also probably blamed it on someone else, which isn't the trait of a great leader.

After that I learned to tell them quickly when we were together that they were terminated and then spend the next hour telling them why so they wouldn't repeat their mistakes and behaviors in their next position. I learned in this job that a big part of my responsibility was to deal with non-performers and to think about all of those people under them who were receiving poor leadership, plus the impact on our guests and the business. My job was not so much about the food and beverage as it was about the people, their performance, their leadership ability and capability.

I went to work one Sunday morning in Chicago after telling Priscilla and Daniel that I would see them in a little while. I did not come home for six weeks. Priscilla brought me clothes and supplies and visited me with Daniel on the weekends. The problems were enormous with the opening, and I had never worked so hard in my life. *It's amazing how things can go from good to bad so fast. At Disney I used to call it going from magic to tragic in the twinkling of an eye.*

It was kind of like 9/11. The day before, September 10, life was so good. I think these tough jobs over the years helped me prepare a lot for what would lie ahead in my career. Once you work in the food and beverage industry for a long time, nothing seems very hard after that. An opening is also an experience everyone should go through.

I learned a lot about myself under this pressure. I learned that I could stay cool and calm, and that had a calming effect on the rest of the team. I learned to be out and about telling people how much I appreciated their efforts, as I was afraid they might quit, frankly. I learned how to be extremely firm and to give orders when I had too. You have to do this more in an opening and during a crisis than at other times in the cycle of a business, it seems. If you don't open right, the place never seems to run correctly after that. Getting it right quickly in an opening is really important. I think that's what Mrs. Marriott was telling me in her own unique way.

Soon enough, we got organized and things ran smoothly. The only big mistake I made was buying that house an hour from the hotel out in Wheaton, Illinois. The real estate agent told me it was only 35 minutes to downtown Chicago; true for Sunday mornings or at 3:00am but not the rest of the days I was driving to work. Plus, the snow and freezing weather added another whole dimension to commuting.

Food and beverage employees have to be at work at all times of the day and night, and that commute caused me to leave work some nights before I should have and to come in later some days than I should have so I could see my family while I could still recognize them. This commute time was very stressful and disruptive to my work and to my personal life.

Since then I have always lived very close to work, so that my commute time was a maximum of 15 minutes. Do you know how bad a VW Bug heater is in the winter in Chicago? You don't want to know. By the way, VW's had no air conditioning either and I learned it's really hot in Chicago in the summer.

An extra two hours a day at home is a big deal. So many people live far away from work to get a nice house and the so-called "good life." They say they do it for their family. That's great if you never want to see your family—or the house—during daylight hours.

When we moved to Paris years later and opened Disneyland Paris, we remembered this lesson. We rented and lived in a 1,000-square-foot apartment on the east side of Paris to be close to work. The really nice, big apartments were on the west side of the city, another 30 minutes driving time from work. While tempting to get that perfect apartment, I remembered the lessons of the past associated with openings. Thank goodness we made that decision with the hours I worked at Disneyland Paris.

Another major thing happened to me in this position in Chicago. Our Director of Marketing, Jon Loeb asked if I would give a speech to 300 convention delegates about the food and beverage business. I agreed and that was my first mistake because I didn't know how to give a speech. Remember, I dropped out of my speech class in college 17 years earlier the day before I would be required to give a speech. I was terrified.

I messed around for a couple of days and wrote out a speech on a yellow pad. I didn't really practice it, and the day quickly came. I walked up on the stage and looked out at those 300 people and knew right then that this was going to be a bad day. I read my speech, and you know how boring that can be … and it was. I rambled on. I really had no main points to make and no business speaking. It was a bad speech, and I could see it on the audience's faces.

I knew they were thinking, "Get this guy out of here, and what in the world is he talking about?" I did not even know how to stop speaking, so I just rambled on and on and on, hoping that if I spoke long enough I would have a heart attack and die to put me out of my misery. My stomach still hurts to this day when I think about it.

The audience was polite and clapped, but I knew the truth. The very next day, I began learning how to give speeches, how to make a point, how to be interesting, and how to use humor.

The best advice I received was from Bill Marriott's father-in-law, Dr. Royal Garff, Professor Emeritus of Speech and Marketing at the University of Utah. He had taught speech and had written a book entitled *You Can Learn to Speak*. He gave me his book and five pieces of advice, and I have followed them ever since. He said, "Lee:

- Don't give speeches … tell stories
- Don't ever give a speech about something that you are not passionate about
- Don't let people write speeches for you
- Always use personal stories to make your point
- Your audience doesn't know what you intended to say, so it does not even matter if you forget something."

This has worked really well for me over the years. Tell stories—don't give speeches—was the lesson. People remember stories. I learned that again when I joined Disney. Storytelling is the name of the game. Everyone loves a good story. And I have added one rule; don't use Power Point. As I tell my clients, "Friends don't let friends use Power Point." I also tell them that my mother did not use it, but rather would say, "Look at me when I am talking to you." Lastly, it's impossible to be inspirational when you use PowerPoint.

One day in late 1979, I got a call 2 years after moving back to Chicago, that someone at Marriott Headquarters in Washington, D.C., wanted to speak with me about a promotion to regional director of food and beverage. His name was Al LeFaivre. He was the first important Al in my life. The second one was Al Weiss my boss at Disney World. Al LeFaivre, Regional Vice President of Marriott Hotels and Resorts came with a background in marketing.

Al Lefaivre checked into the Chicago Marriott without my knowledge and tested the food and beverage operation for three days to see what kind of operation I was running. He checked the food, the service, sanitation, maintenance, and many other things in all of the restaurants, banquets, bars, and room service. He told me in the interview that he already knew how good I was, *"Your operation is a reflection of YOU."*

I never forgot that. Your annual performance rating cannot be higher than your operations performance.

In my first book, *Creating Magic,* one of the chapters recommends doing just this before you hire people. Go check out their operation to see if they are as good as they tell you they are. They are only as good as the results they achieve.

In Chapter 6, I tell you a little more about the next part of my career development and the good things—and the not-so-good things in my next position. I was about to leave Chicago for Washington, D.C., with *$5 million dollars in experience, but little in the bank.* At least by now we had opened a savings account. Financially things are starting to look up after 15 years in the workplace.

We decided to give the yellow VW Bug to Priscilla's brother, Hank, who needed a car. We had been driving it for 7 years. We took the white VW with us, or the silver VW as I called it when I used valet parking at a fancy restaurant. Asking for the silver VW always seemed to sound better than asking for the white one. It was like asking for the silver Bentley or Rolls Royce.

I now have been working for 15 years. I am 35 years old. Daniel is almost 11 and only 7 years away from college tuition! *Yikes!*

The one thing I realize now is that I still had at least another 30 years to work so maybe I was not in as much trouble financially and career wise as I thought I was. Too bad we can't see forward as well as we can see backward!

5

NINE YEARS OF PROMOTIONS, TRAVEL & DISAPPOINTMENT

1979–1988

THE OPENING of the Chicago Marriott was a really great experience and prepared me in many ways for my next position in Washington, D.C., at the Marriott Headquarters.

It was November 1979 and as previously mentioned I had been working almost 15 years. I am now 35-years-old. Daniel is almost 11 and only 7 years away from college tuition. We don't really have much in savings. Living in all of these very expensive cities did not leave much for the "old" savings account or investments. Every vacation to date had been by car to stay with and visit family or friends; that's all we could afford. In those days we could have never afforded a trip to Disney World.

I have just finished my 15th job since 1964. We were about to make our eighth move to Washington, D.C. Priscilla is happy since it's where she grew up and I'm happy since it's where I started my professional career, and I like Washington a lot. Daniel is not happy since he does not want to leave his fourth-grade pals in Chicago. He was unhappy for about two weeks. If we all got over things as fast as children do, we would be much better off.

My new role would be the regional director of food and beverage operations for Marriott Hotels and Resorts for the East Coast. I will now be working with a regional team of executives and report to a regional vice president of operations. This would be my first executive-level position.

Remember we gave away the yellow VW Bug to Priscilla's brother? This new position came with a company car. I told you that every job has good things and things that are not so good. I told you before that I thought I had a name for this, *"perks and anti-perks."* I sometimes think that they cancel each other out. This car was a nice perk. The anti-perk turned out to be that I would be traveling five days a week and away from home Monday through Friday almost every single week.

Another anti-perk was not being able to have dinner with my family at night or having breakfast with them in the morning. It was also tough as I was very tired when I got home on Friday evenings after barely catching the last flight from some Northeastern city like Boston or New York in a raging snowstorm. A perk though was that the salary was quite a bit better however the cost of housing and other things in Washington were also quite a bit higher than Chicago. Perk, anti-perk, perk, anti-perk.

Being in a corporate headquarters staff role was a completely different role for me since I had been in operations for 15 years. We were a team made up of a regional vice president, director of marketing and sales, finance, rooms division, human resources, and food and beverage. In this position, I did not have any official authority over the directors of food and beverage in the hotels up and down the East Coast. They reported directly to the general managers of each hotel. I was supposed to get my job done through influence and expertise. This turned out to be a bit of a challenge since my management style at the time was to get things done by telling people what to do and using my authority or intimidation to get it done.

At first I did not do as great a job of partnering in this new position with the general managers, as I should have. I did get better at this though, as I figured out that I needed them on my side to get my job done. You see, no one had talked to me yet about leadership, partnering, and all of the things that I have written about in my book, *Creating Magic: 10 Common Sense Leadership Strategies from a Life at Disney.*

Oh, how I wish I had had that book back in those days.

Much of what I wrote in *Creating Magic* was because of my ability to reflect on the successes and mistakes that I had made along my career journey, as well as observing the behaviors of both great and poor leaders.

I was technically excellent. I was an awesome manager, meaning I was organized and could make things happen. There were no deadlines I could not meet and those I worked with knew that. They also knew that they better meet them too whether they reported to me or not. My nickname was Doberman, I found out years later. Today I am a Cocker Spaniel. I can bite, but I don't and I don't even growl that often.

I completed my responsibilities as the regional director of food and beverage without fail. I did it by sheer drive and a touch of intimidation. I get things accomplished quite differently today.

I did get results, though and I received the top rating every year on my annual performance review, so I was receiving positive reinforcement for my management style.

You see this is the problem. If a person is not behaving properly and you give that person a top rating, then you are the one making the problem more serious and you're also hurting that person's future because *bad behaviors always catch up with you sooner or later.* Read the front page of the paper every morning. Every story is about failed leadership and bad leadership behaviors. Go ahead, go get the paper and take a look. Every day it is right there on the front page. These stories are in the local section too—and even on the sports page—and for sure in the business section. I'm sure they are even in the classifieds. An entire cartoon series, *Dilbert* by Scott Adams, was inspired by poor leadership behaviors … and he will never run out of material.

In this new role we traveled as a team every week and would visit one or two hotels and audit their performance. We would check everything for compliance. We would find many things wrong and these visits were very stressful for the hotels. When a Doberman approaches you, I'm pretty sure you experience some stress.

Later on, I tried a different approach. I would tell the hotels thirty to sixty days before my visit what I was going to audit and check up on. This gave them time to get their act together. In 30–60 days, they had adopted new operating guidelines and practices. The important things were being done correctly.

Now I would come and find things right. They learned from this process, and we had a good visit with far less stress. By this time I was a mixed breed. I was half Doberman and half Cocker Spaniel. Upon the next visit I would give them a list of other things to focus on. As the years went on, I became more of a Cocker Spaniel and less of a Doberman. I transitioned from being a boss to being a teacher.

The lesson here is that looking for what's right is far more productive than only looking for what's wrong.

Our team would sit together with the hotel management team at the beginning and end of the visit and decide on priorities. We would usually come back in three months and go over the priorities to make sure they were getting done. We made lots of progress with this approach. We always left the hotels with a list of measurable priorities for them to work on accompanied by reachable deadlines.

Priscilla and I bought a house in Rockville, Maryland, a suburb of Washington, D.C. The recession of 1980 was in full gear, and interest rates were going up a half-point a day because this recession had both runaway inflation and unemployment problems. The Federal Reserve was trying to get inflation under control before it dealt with the unemployment problem, so everyone felt the pain. I don't think Jimmy Carter was having a whole lot of fun over at the White House.

We finally closed at 11½% on our mortgage and felt lucky at that. We had an 8% mortgage back in Chicago so quickly much of the increase in salary disappeared to higher interest payments on the mortgage. Mortgage rates eventually rose to 20% in 1980. When that happened our mortgage rate looked pretty good, but our rate was still in the category of anti-perk as was the 7% local income tax in Montgomery Country, Maryland. Real estate taxes as well were much higher as were many things in the Washington, D.C., area.

One really nice perk was that we had stumbled into a really nice neighborhood with nice neighbors who had nice kids. I learn a lot by watching the behaviors of children, and I got another lesson while the moving van was unloading our furniture into our new home. The doorbell rang, and I opened the door and there was a group of little boys standing there. The obvious leader of the group looked up at us and said, "Hi, I am Bobby Reiger. Do you have any kids?" I said, "Yes, we do, but he is not here yet. He will be here in two weeks as he is still in Chicago staying with his friends there." Bobby said, "Okay, we will be back!"

The lesson here is that *if adults could learn to be as outgoing and direct they would have new friends very quickly when they moved.* These kids were 9 years old. To a 9-year-old, a moving van signals the possibility of a new friend. To an adult, it signals things like, "I wonder who they are and if we will like them," "I wonder what he or she does," or "I hope they are nice." Kids don't wonder—they act! Even today 38 years later Daniel is still friends with James Toth, Arnie Pike and Mark Surette. We see them and their families often.

Another great perk was that the house we bought was nine minutes from my office in a great school district. The anti-perk was that I was usually not going to my office but to the airport, which was 45 minutes away because of the infamously traffic-clogged Beltway in Washington. A perk was that Daniel could walk to elementary school, middle school, and high school and Priscilla thought this was a great perk. Yes in those days parents actually let their kids walk to school.

Priscilla's dad, Admiral Payne (Charlie) called one day and said he would like to give us his old company car, a 4-year-old Chrysler, from the shipyard he was running in Texas after retiring from a 32-year Navy career. All I had to do was fly to Dallas, pick up the car and drive it back. This sounded good. I flew down to Dallas and picked it up and we got rid of our last VW Bug. I did receive one good lesson on the drive back from Texas to Washington.

A Texas Ranger State Trooper stopped me in the middle of

nowhere while I was driving through Texas. He came up to the car and said very politely, "Good afternoon, sir. May I ask if you have an emergency?" I said, "No, sir." He said, "Okay then, you just sit right here while I write out your speeding ticket." This Trooper was cool. His professional composure and his asking just that one question impressed me. I was not even upset at getting the ticket. I am sure that if I would have had a good reason to be speeding, he would have assisted me and not given me that ticket. The lesson is obvious … *always stay professional.* He gave me the ticket and said, "Now you be careful and have a nice day." He was so nice he could have worked at Disney World. *Always remember that it is not what you say or do that upsets people so much as how you say it. Choose your words carefully. As my grandson Jullian reminded me, your tongue is one of the strongest muscles in the body. Be careful how you use it or you might hurt someone.*

Priscilla now had a big car. The anti-perk, this car never ran right … but it was free. If it rained, it would not start. And sometimes it would not start when the sun was shining.

I am telling you that you really need to study my Perk and Anti-Perk theory. I think I coined this phrase since I have never heard it before. Walt said a lot of things so I want to start to say more so when I am gone people will say, "Lee said that." Walt said better things, though, I think. Most people think too much about what they don't have instead of being thankful for what they do have.

One big thing I learned in a traveling job was to call home every night, but don't always tell your wife what you had for dinner. We had great dinners on the road while Priscilla was home trying to raise Daniel and often eating grilled-cheese or tuna fish sandwiches. The hotel business was a good perk for meals. Part of my responsibilities was to eat in the best restaurants in each city. The anti-perk was my waistline growth if I didn't watch it. Actually, I started working out regularly when I was 27. Being in food and beverage industry, you can put on a few pounds each year before you know it. I was actually jogging even before it was commonplace and the cool thing to do. I was jogging before jogging shoes cost more than anything else in your wardrobe. Working out regularly is a good lesson for you. Today I weigh what I did when I got out of the army at 20 years old. I weight myself every morning, I look up the calories on the web for what I am about to eat, I try to eat 400 or less calories for breakfast and another 500 or less for lunch. This leaves me enough to have a nice dinner and some wine. I do weight training twice a week and walk or jog almost every day. Implement this habit in your life now! It takes a lot of energy to be a leader and to work long hours when you have to. The difference between feeling good and feeling great is *huge*.

Another thing I learned was to make a reservation to take Priscilla out to dinner when I got home on Friday night instead of falling asleep on the couch and waking up just in time to go to bed. This routine is really bad for a marriage and still, unfortunately, practiced by many couples even today.

This was the year I received a memo from my boss, George Washko, that I had to attend a mandatory time management seminar. The memo said it would be for two days, and it would be eight hours each day. I resisted and tried to talk my way out of going. I said, "I don't have time to go to a two-day seminar on time management."

This is the wrong thing to say to your boss about the subject of time management. If you don't have the time, then you probably need it. That's like saying I don't have time to work out and stay fit, but the end result of this decision is an early departure from this life.

I resisted going so much because I thought I was organized. I got my work in on time, and I always received a great performance rating.

What I learned in the time management seminar was unbelievable. I believe it was a key that has helped me during my entire life since 1980. It was the best seminar I ever attended. Once again this time management seminar taught me that I don't know everything. This has been a recurring problem in my career. I think I am over it now. *I now know that you really never know it all.* In fact, it is pretty arrogant to even think you could, so listen and you'll learn new things that will make you an even better leader in all areas of your life.

In this time management seminar:

- I learned that I was working far too many hours and too many weekends and nights to get my work done.

- I learned how to think about priorities versus doing everything.

- I learned how to get big projects done by involving others and through effective delegation.

- I learned how to focus on family and friends, and how to lead one life and not think about your life as your business life and your personal life. One life is hard enough to lead without trying to lead two.

I learned the concept of scheduling the priorities in your life and that is why I started to schedule dinner out with Priscilla every Friday night when I got home. I was still tired, but going out together while talking about the week and how Daniel was doing and just a quiet evening together made all of the difference in the world with our relationship. We often just went to a small inn nearby and had a hamburger and some wine. From time to time, we went to a fancy place, but the inn, I think, was really our favorite. The inn was casual, quiet, and close to home, plus after a while we were regulars and when you are a regular, the whole experience gets better and better. The lesson here is *treat all of your customers as regulars and they might well become regulars.*

The concept of scheduling the priorities in your life is an important one. This is why I have all of my workouts scheduled every day in my calendar. When I didn't schedule them, I did not get a regular workout in but when I made them appointments in my calendar, I made real progress. I wanted to get to retirement and beyond alive so, of course, staying fit is one-third of the formula, eating right is one-third, and getting enough sleep is one-third. Don't even think about smoking or being around people that smoke!

I would be really angry if I paid all of that Social Security for 40 to 50 years and never got to collect any of it. At the least, you should set a goal of getting to retirement *alive*. Right now, I'm collecting my social security and plan to do so for a long, long time.

I learned a lot of other things in that time management seminar too and if you want to learn these things, then pick up my book, *Time Management Magic: How to Get More Done, Every Day and Move from Surviving to Thriving.* Learning to manage your life is a vital unless you enjoy having your life a total mess. This system will keep your life under control, which is ultimately what time management is all about. Spend the time planning the life you want or spend a lot of time later leading a life you don't want.

Another thing happened to me in this period of my career. I learned about a seminar that was being taught on service at the University of Kentucky, so I signed up for this two-day seminar. It was called "Service America" and was taught by the author of the book by the same name.

The guts of the seminar dealt with how to manage a service business, just like manufacturing companies manage quality control on a manufacturing assembly line. This seminar put to rest the theory, at that time, that service businesses were hit-and-miss on how good the service could really be on a consistent basis.

The seminar focused on how you don't have to depend on luck to have good service. Service businesses have key points of contact and services that are more critical than others such as employee selection, training, and audit. You can read the book if you are interested in learning more about this approach to managing a service business.

This seminar got me very excited about how we could improve service consistency with the right processes, expectations, education, and enforcement. This seminar and the time-management seminar were a defining moment in altering my management style and approach to both my business and personal responsibilities. These two seminars led to my deep interest in leadership, and I started to read and study everything I could get my hands on about it. Two other books that made an impact on me were, *The One Minute Manager* by Ken Blanchard and *7 Habits of Highly Effective People* by Stephen Covey. I'm still reading and I'm about to start reading the book *From Zero to One* by Peter Thiel and Blake Masters. I started to see the leadership triumphs and failures in every story in the newspaper and weekly magazines. These lessons started to jump out of the television and off the pages of the paper like they never had before. I really wanted to understand more about the impact one individual could make in causing the right things to happen. The *Service America* book and seminar taught me one thing that has really stuck with me all of these years. I use the concept every day to get work done and to think about how we are doing.

"The Moment of Truth" is defined as the moment that the guests/customers/patients/students/passengers, etc. come into contact with a company's product or people. What happens at this moment is the name of the game. This is where expectation and reality meet. The guests/customers come with a level of expectation that has been formed in their minds by marketing and advertising campaigns, word of mouth, sales pitches, or past visits. Even they themselves, develop their own expectations, by growing their expectation in their own minds to a level that's far beyond what we might even have in mind for their experience.

Marketing's job is to create the expectation, and it is our job in operations to execute it so well that we meet or exceed that expectation. When operations exceeds the customer's expectation that sets up an expectation for their next visit which means, at a minimum, we have to perform consistently and hopefully improve.

I started teaching the concepts of moments of truth, time management, and leadership and quickly learned that, when you teach you learn. *Teaching puts you on the spot to perform better. You can't stand up and teach and then not walk the talk.* I learned that any time I want to force myself to do something, all I have to do is to get in front of a few groups and tell them what I stand for and what I plan to do. This simple concept drives me to get it done.

If leaders don't walk the talk, then they quickly are not taken seriously and worst of all, they soon have no followers. Without followers and a constituency, you are a leader in name only.

It was not long before I was thought of as an expert in time management, leadership, and service-management. It is interesting how you can get this kind of reputation by just focusing on a few things and learning everything you can about those subjects. I think that I have read every book on leadership and management that was ever published. I then began to teach these seminars all over the world to all Marriott employees and even outside groups. I learned many great lessons from these two seminars that I attended. Becoming an expert in these areas turned out even better in the long run as I taught these same concepts to thousands of Disney Cast Members and today have a very successful and profitable business teaching these same concepts around the world to organizations of all sizes. These two seminars even helped me become a successful author.

After I became really good at practicing the time management system, I began teaching the seminar to help others become more organized and also to improve my public speaking skills. This was good because then I could practice on my fellow employees with whom I was more comfortable.

I always wonder how many people go to a seminar or a class and then never do anything with what they have learned. Many, I think. One thing that really bothers me is seeing individuals give up on themselves way too early—not trying harder and being more persistent—to attain their goals and dreams. *"Never, Never, Never Give Up"* as Winston Churchill said.

In the book, *7 Habits of Highly Effective People* by Stephen R. Covey, one of the "7 habits" is called *Sharpening the Saw*. This simply means that if you want to get better performance out of yourself, then you need to sharpen your skills and knowledge, just like one sharpens a saw to get better performance out of it. Going to seminars, reading, and getting hands-on experience is sharpening the saw. Are you sharp or dull? When was the last time you sharpened your saw? Remember, you can't just sharpen the saw once unless you never plan to use it again and if that is the case, why sharpen it in the first place? The best way to hurt yourself is by using a dull knife. A dull knife is more dangerous than a sharp one because you have to use more force.

When I visited the Marriott hotels over the next few years, I would audit them and teach a time management, service management, and leadership class, which helped the staff become better leaders and managers. This time also gave them an opportunity to get to know me better on a more personal level. I was now providing them with the knowledge and tools they needed to do a better job. When you do this, you are really making a difference. Teaching is the name of the game for leaders if you want to leave a legacy. Teaching comes in many forms, including in the classroom, walking around observing and correcting, and by simply setting a good example. We all remember the great teachers in our lives. I guess that is why Priscilla has said to me for 48 years, "Lee, be careful what you say and do today. They are watching you and judging you." This goes for all of us. Role modeling is the best teacher of all, at work and at home. Just remember your children and fellow team members are always watching and listening. They don't learn their values by what you say; they learn them by what you do.

I run into people all over the world who come up to me and tell me that they were in one of my time-management classes 20 years ago and how it's helped them. One lady told me that my class saved her marriage. She was so glad that her husband had attended.

Others tell me how they changed after that seminar and how it propelled their careers and helped them in their personal lives as well. I love hearing this feedback from people I've helped by teaching them something that I have learned. This is where the true satisfaction of leadership comes from, for me anyway. *A leader's job is to produce more leaders. A parent's job is to produce children whom can become great parents, citizens and leaders as well.* I even had Daniel attend my time management seminar with a couple of his buddies before he went off to Boston University. I told him I was only paying for 4 years so he needed to be organized, attend class, sit on the front row in every class and tell the professors they are doing a good job. When the professor knows you and knows you appreciate them they may give you a small benefit of the doubt and raise your grade. This is how real life works. People can't help you if they don't know you. Don't sit in the back.

I held this regional director of food and beverage position at Marriott from 1979 to 1984. I opened more than 100 hotels during this period, and it was travel, travel and more travel. Much of my time was spent recruiting new people into the company as we were growing by leaps and bounds. You really learn how important talent is during a time like this. I so wish that back then I had known about using structured interviews that we learned from Jan Miller at the Gallup organization a few years ago at Disney and from my partner Carol Quinn on how to ask the right question and what to listen for in the answers. Carol's website is www.HireAuthority.com if you are interested in becoming an expert in interviewing and hiring. Mention my name and she might give you an even better deal. At the very least study her book, *Don't Hire Anyone Without Me.*

These structured interviews help you understand how people think which is what you want to know before you hire them. Just by using the normal interview process, I hired a lot of wrong-fit talent back in those days. I asked far too many questions back then that could be answered by a yes-or-no answer. We were opening a hotel every two weeks, so I was hiring just about anyone I spoke to. Today I have learned how to hire right-fit talent and seldom make any major errors.

In 1984 I was promoted to area vice president of hotel food and beverage, and my responsibilities included half of all of the Marriott Hotels and Resorts in the United States. This job too was travel, travel, and more travel. The title vice president was the perk with an increase in salary. The anti-perk continued to be the nonstop travel. A really good perk was that I was learning a lot through the experiences I was involved in with this position.

During this time we focused on improving Marriott's convention and catering business, and our goal was to be the best at it of all major hotel chains. We accomplished that mission over the next few years through setting new standards for service and equipment, hiring the right people, and through education (training), and enforcement. We continued with rapid hotel openings at the same time. At least in those days, flying was tolerable; you could get to the airport sixty seconds before your flight and not miss it. This was a mini-perk compared to traveling today.

Once again, one of the major errors I made in this position was that I didn't take the time to cultivate a good relationship with the regional vice presidents of the different divisions of Marriott. I was out there literally forcing a lot of changes the way I saw fit. I hit the ground running and was totally focused on getting things done when I should have gotten the relationships right before I started with the tactics. These regional vice presidents were in positions above me in the organization's structure and had a lot of influence, which I found out later to my detriment. It wasn't that I was doing anything wrong, but whether we like it or not there is a political angle that one cannot forget in life. It is just the way it is and it's never going to change. People above you can hurt your career even if they themselves are incompetent.

You put a lot of ambitious, smart individuals together; the competition with one another begins. Sometimes it is in small, hard-to-notice ways and sometimes it is in big destructive ways. Often, I believe, people don't realize how different their behaviors are at work versus in their personal lives with their family and friends. As someone once said, "You need a healthy ego to be successful, but you need to learn to check it at the door." *There is a big difference between a healthy ego and being egotistical.*

Relationships matter. Don't ever forget this. If you are a great performer, technically competent, and a great manager, but you don't have strong political and relational skills; you risk failure or, at a minimum, disappointment. Leaders who have good one-on-one relationships and good multi-relationships are simply more successful and able to get more things accomplished. This concept is not rocket science, but many people find it extremely difficult to live by. Go for the win-win when you can and not just the win for you at any cost. As they say, *"Save your bullets for the really big battles."*

This phenomenon happens at every level. There are perfectly normal, nice people who become weird when they come to work. A lot of it has to do with insecurity and greed. A lot of it has to do with an ego that turns the person into becoming egotistical and self-centered and a lot of it has to do with selfish ambition along with many other reasons. It's a sad thing and the people doing it usually never figure out that people are laughing and talking about them behind their backs. I have worked with very senior people like this at Hilton, Marriott, Disney and run into them frequently in my own business today. One of the frequent comments I receive from attendees of my leadership seminars is, "My boss needs your seminar badly." There is a big difference between what you do, how much money you make, and who you really are.

Make sure that you have the same leadership style and behaviors both up the chain of command and down the chain of command. If you don't, people will know and you lose credibility. Have you ever seen leaders who are totally different in front of their boss than they are in front of their direct reports? The people who report to you see the real you, and we all need to make sure that that is the way our boss sees us as well.

I know I have been there more than once—earlier in my career—in not understanding the importance of good relationship skills. Does that make me a fool? Yes, it does! I have become much better in this area over the last several years. Today I am "me" … 24 hours a day … for better or worse. It is way too hard to have different personalities especially when your boss and your direct reports are in the same room. Actually, I can think of many people I have worked with who need to get treated for having multiple personalities. If you know anyone with this problem, you may want to recommend to that person to use his or her medical plan to get the correct medication to overcome this multiple personality disorder by seeing a mental health specialist.

The bottom lines is that *if people don't like you or trust you, then you are not going to get very far and you will never quite know why because they may never tell you.* It really is common sense; but as we know, common sense is less and less common. Even if you get a big job with these traits, people will never respect you … and that, for me would not be worth the high-level job attained.

All you have is your own reputation in life. I want my family, friends and colleagues to remember me as a good man rather than a selfish, attain-success-at-any-cost, nut! I have reformed since I started out in business many years ago. If I kept going the way I did in my early days I would be the only one at my funeral one day.

In November 1985, I was promoted to vice president, food and beverage planning for all Marriott Hotels and Resorts around the world. This was a very interesting job because I got to plan the hotel food and beverage operations from the ground up. I got to travel all over the world, and I learned a lot working on projects in places like Hong Kong, Mexico, Poland, and so many others. When you travel, you really grow in knowledge and wisdom.

I learned in Hong Kong how great service could be. I experienced service there like nowhere else I had ever been. That is why today I believe that you cannot provide service better than what you have experienced. It is critical to travel and get out and about to experience the world so that you will know what is possible. Knowing what is possible can drive you to achieve higher and higher levels of excellence. Get out into the world and see it, touch it, hear it, smell it and taste it! This experience is far different than reading about it or watching a program about it on TV or your computer.

I was so impressed with the service in Asia that Priscilla and I took Daniel there when he graduated from high school in 1987 to add to his education. We spent a month in Japan, Hong Kong, and China; and this trip left us with lasting impressions that I know changed a lot of the ways the three of us think today. This is what experience and travel does. It changes you. It opens your eyes and mind to the possibilities in life. People often ask me, what was the one thing I did that contributed most to my success. The answer? I got out of the little town I grew up in and experienced what was happening in the rest of the world. So far I have visited 36 countries and had both unbelievable and valuable experiences in every single one of them. Travel is the very best way to overcome bigotry as well.

I went to Mexico once to do research on two hotel projects for Marriott. The man who picked me up in Puerto Vallarta did not speak one word of English, and I did not speak more than three words of Spanish. He and I somehow spent three days together and got our work done and had a great time. Somehow we communicated. We both showed each other pictures of our sons. This is what we had in common and what we were both proud of. *The lesson I learned here is that there is always "common ground," if you look for it.*

I worked on a Marriott hotel project in Warsaw, Poland, before the Berlin Wall came down. When I landed in Warsaw, there were police everywhere with automatic weapons. If you have not experienced this, I can assure you that it leaves a lasting impression about the wonderful freedoms we have in America. When I met with the local people on the construction project, there was always a Communist Party member present to listen to the conversations. I was offered vodka at 9:00am at our first meeting, and I said, "No, thanks." He said, "You don't drink?" (In those days I was not drinking any alcohol.) I said, "No," and he said, "Never?" I had a cup of coffee, and I think that for the rest of the trip this man thought there was something seriously wrong with me. We went to lunch at 3:00pm and dinner at 10:00pm, which is the local custom in Poland. I love wine now, but I stop drinking alcoholic beverages for a few weeks several times a year just to make sure I can. This is called self-discipline.

I completed my research on possible concepts for the Warsaw Marriott. Before leaving Poland I had a final meeting with the local team and told them I was going to create an all-day dining café, and it would be named after a famous Polish Poet. They liked that. I told them we would also do a grillroom concept for steaks and chops and things like that, and I asked them if we could name it the American Grill.

The Communist Party member about had a heart attack and excitedly said, "No, no. You cannot use words that have America in them." I then said, "Okay, what about California Grill?" and he said, "No. That is too close to Reagan." You see, at that time Ronald Reagan was the President of the United States and was from California. I then knew I had the right name for him. I had lived in Chicago twice, and I knew that Chicago had more Polish immigrants than any place in the world. I said, "What about, Chicago Grill?" and a big smile came over his face and he said, "Yes. Chicago good. Many Polish people in Chicago." So the Chicago Grill at the Warsaw Marriott was born.

I learned a lot about diversity and inclusiveness in this job, traveling around the world to do my work. When you travel and get to know the people, you find out that people everywhere are the same. They are just trying to have a decent life, trying to make things better for their children and they are proud of their families, their religion, their culture, and their country.

I spent a lot of time in libraries doing research on food concepts for places all over the world since the Internet was in its infancy and there were no search engines like Google. I still like to go to the library for a few hours to work, as it's a great place to think and dream. No one bothers you and the librarians are very knowledgeable and helpful. On business trips today when I want a quiet place to work, I go to the public library. You can even use their computers if you don't want to drag yours along.

The day finally came when I learned that my boss, Karl Kilburg, Senior Vice President of Food and Beverage, was going to become a regional vice president and run a region of hotels for Marriott. He held the position that I was always sure I would get one day. I was more than qualified for it, and I could think of no reason why I would not be promoted when it became open.

Well, the subtle hints started to come to me that I would probably not get the job. Everyone danced around it for months until one day Karl finally told me the truth. I was told that I would not get the job because some of the regional vice presidents did not support me for the years I ran roughshod over them to get things done. By the way, this was the very first time that I had heard this comment. I had all top annual ratings, and this had never been discussed with me. Don't count on someone always telling you the truth. Don't be naïve.

Anyway, five regional vice presidents supported me and four did not. I happened to see the list that was on Karl's desk, as I can read upside down very well. There was a yes or no by each name. I spent the next few months fixing my relationship problem with those four who did not support me. Since I was not going to get the big job, I told Karl that I wanted to go be the general manager of a hotel and to leave Marriott Headquarters. There was no way I could stay and work for someone else.

I can tell you that during this time I was not a "happy camper." I started going home early and not putting a lot of effort into my work. I was very disappointed and angry about not getting the job. I was probably suffering from mild depression too. My last disappointment had been 15 years before when I was fired. I had had a run of 15 years of promotion after promotion and success after success. Remember that career roller coaster I told you about? I was about to get another ride on the "Big-Drop Career Coaster," which is unsettling to your stomach and makes Rock 'n' Roller Coaster at Disney look like child's play.

They at first told me "No" to the general manager's position and by now you know that I don't like the word no very much. They told me I would have to be a resident manager first. I went professionally ballistic, and they soon offered me a general manager's job in the smallest hotel in the company in Springfield, Massachusetts. The hotel was small, old, and had not been renovated in years.

I accepted the job. I'm sure they thought I would quit, but I didn't. I had been in the hotel business for 23 years, but I had not managed a hotel. I thought taking a step-down was a good idea and would give me more opportunities for the future. At the moment things didn't look great for my career, but that trusty roller coaster soon started back up, and the ride was to be more exciting than I could ever have imagined. Little did I know that, that coaster was on its way to a Magic Kingdom and The Walt Disney Company.

I am now 44 years old. Daniel is 19 and in his first year at Boston University. I have been working for 24 years. I have been married for 20 years. Priscilla and I are about to make our ninth move since we were married. This last assignment was good because Daniel started fourth grade in Rockville, Maryland, and then went on to college without any relocation during that time. This was a major perk for our family.

I had earned many millions in experience during these last 8 years. I had achieved several promotions. I had been a vice president for 4 years, and now I was going off to learn how to manage a hotel. By now I even had some money in the bank and some investments in the stock market.

In Chapter 6, I'll tell you about my new adventure as the general manager of a hotel and how this move turned out to be one of the most important moves of my career.

6

GENERAL MANAGER
1988–1990

S O HERE IT WAS, 1988, and I have been working for 24 years in the hotel business. All 24 years were in food and beverage. I started as a banquet server, and I rose to the level of vice president. I was sure that my next promotion would be to senior vice president of food and beverage for the Marriott Corporation, but it was not to be as previously mentioned. My career is starting to feel like one of those pogo sticks that go up and down.

I thought long and hard about my situation and decided that for my future it would be in my best interest to become a general manager of a hotel. I successfully negotiated that deal with one of the regional vice presidents.

We had been living in Washington, D.C., for 8 years; and frankly we thought we would never leave there. We loved our home, our neighborhood, and our friends. We had family living in the area as well. Daniel had grown up in that house from fourth grade to college. Things were quite perfect until this blip in my career.

The hotel that I was assigned to was the Springfield, Massachusetts, Marriott. This was the smallest hotel in the company. It had been another brand of hotel, but was taken over by Marriott a few years earlier. It was old, run down, and small (250 rooms). It was owned by the Mass Mutual Insurance Company, which had its headquarters in Springfield.

Priscilla and I took a trip up to Springfield on a weekend to take a look at it before we relocated there. When we walked into the hotel, Priscilla said to me: "Lee, what did you do to deserve this place? What did you do to those people back at headquarters?"

All we could do was laugh. The alternative was to cry! *Don't assume that someone laughing is happy.*

We went back to Washington at the end of the weekend. My boss Karl Kilburg had a nice going-away party for me and said many kind things about how great I was. You all know how it goes. When you are leaving, everyone loves you. He said, "Lee is great and one of our best leaders. He is personally responsible for much of our success over the last few years." (I was thinking, "and that is why they gave me the Springfield Marriott?") He didn't say this, but I thought it. I made my thank-you speech and was very professional. I said that I was very excited to have this opportunity and really appreciated all of the support I was receiving blah, blah, blah … at least by now I had learned how not to burn bridges as I did earlier in my career.

By the way, I do believe that I was at least 51% responsible for the different difficulties that I have experienced in my career. I don't blame it all on others, and could say that I didn't receive feedback or help on my leadership behaviors, but *there are some things in life that you need to figure out for yourself.* We are in an age where it seems as if everyone wants to blame someone else for his or her circumstances or sue someone for something. However, much of the time, we are responsible for the situations we find ourselves in.

People want to blame the government, the weather, their boss, their partner, their wife, their husband, their mother, their father, their sister, their genetic make-up, and on and on. No one seems to want to blame him or herself, which is where most of the blame really lies.

Priscilla and I decided that I would go ahead to Springfield; she would visit on weekends and move in about three months. At the time she had a lot of things to take care of and she was working for a friend, who needed her. Dan and Pat Pewett were some of our best and most trusted friends in Washington. Pat passed away from cancer several years ago but we still make sure we see Dan and spend time with him a couple of times a year.

One thing I seem to be really good at is not being in town on moving day. Priscilla says that I do it on purpose. We have moved a lot, and I just always seem to have an important meeting on moving day. "It's not my fault," I always told her with a grin.

This worked out perfectly because I moved into the Springfield Marriott hotel and lived there for three months. When you live, eat, and sleep in the hotel, you manage to learn a lot very quickly and actually you learn a lot of things that you would have never learned if you did not live there. I learned that it took 10 minutes for hot water to arrive to the 14th floor of the hotel at 5:00am where my room was. I kept a hot-water time log each day because my Director of Engineering did not believe me. He soon believed me when I personally climbed into the ceiling and found a recirculation line that had the valve shut. I just wonder how long this had been going on and how many guests had suffered because of this problem and how much compensation we had given out. This turned out to be the beginning of the end for my Director of Engineering. *Where there is smoke, there is fire.*

I took my Day-Timer® planner and wrote down everything I could think of that I wanted to know about the hotel. Every day for the first month I would meet with my department heads and ask them the questions I had. If they knew the answer, they told me. If they didn't, they told me the next day or as soon as they could find the answer. I told them it was okay not to know the answers, but please don't make the answers up.

Some advice I received years before was that when you arrive at a new position, take the time in the first thirty days to write down everything you see that seems like it is wrong or needs improving and then spend your time there fixing those issues. After the first month or two, you won't see things anymore like you will when you first get there. I wanted to know things like:

- How much is our maintenance budget?
- What are the electric costs each year?
- What are the water costs each year?
- How many people work in each department, and what are their responsibilities?
- What are the food costs?
- What was the profit of the hotel last year?
- What are our costs related to employee accidents?
- What is our accident frequency?

This process got me up to speed very quickly, and it made me more observant as I dealt with issues and made observations around the property each day.

I personally approved and signed off on all of the invoices for all departments so I could become familiar with what we were buying and what every single thing was costing. This is a very productive and informative thing to do. If you control the spending, then you control the profit.

Things as simple as when tomatoes became too expensive, I asked the chef to remove the tomatoes from the salad until they came down in price. During the '80s when McDonald's® introduced a burger with tomatoes on it, tomato prices went through the roof for a while. You learn these things from reading the paper every morning by the way.

I told my engineer not to use several outside services anymore when I saw the cost, and I had him work up for me a reduced-cost solution. You will be amazed what will trigger your mind when you see the cost and quantities of the different things you are buying. Review every single invoice in your business and you will be amazed at what you learn.

In the first week, I went around and asked each department head what one thing he or she most wanted for their department was.

- Housekeeping told me they wanted a new carpet in the lobby, as the one there was embarrassing.
- The banquet staff told me they needed more hangers for the coatroom. I sent one of them right to the store to buy them that very minute and to bring me the receipt.
- The restaurant team told me that they needed more silverware and that they needed to have more fresh fish on the menu. We ordered the flatware that day and started two fresh fish specials on the following Monday.

The owners of the hotel, Mass Mutual Insurance Company, told me they hated the plastic flowers over the revolving door in the lobby. I had them removed that night.

I did this for every single department. I wanted to show each department immediate movement on getting them what they needed to do their jobs.

Putting that rug in the lobby made me famous with the staff. You would have thought I had renovated the entire hotel. When they asked for something really big or too expensive, I got back to them with an answer on when we might be able to do that or told them the reason why we would not be able to do it. Telling people "why" is really important. I gained a lot of credibility and quick wins with the staff by doing this. By this time in my career, I had learned to ask questions, listen more, talk less and take quick action.

I joined the Springfield Convention and Visitors Bureau. I went to the Rotary Club meeting every Friday. I was on the Board of the Chamber of Commerce. I established an excellent relationship with the mayor, our local congressman, and the owners of the hotel, Mass Mutual. Our hotel was downtown, so these relationships were important. I had never been involved much in the community before, so there were lots of good, learning opportunities for me in this role and in a small community you can't hide! *You have to participate and be involved. Get involved with your community!*

Priscilla got involved with a literacy program. She would make me hire her students as soon as she taught them to read. *"A job builds self-confidence and self-esteem,"* she would tell me and she kept the pressure on me to find a place for these people who had the drive to get ahead.

One of her students was a woman who had never traveled far from home because she literally could not find her way back. She signed up with Priscilla for classes when one day her kids asked her to make cookies, and she could not read the recipe.

She also wanted to be able to read a story to them before they went to sleep. She went on to get her driver's license and a job, and her life improved dramatically. She was illiterate in English and Spanish. She could speak both but could not read until she got connected with Priscilla. The community expected both of us to be involved, and we were. The satisfaction one gets from teaching someone else to read is enormous. Priscilla even received an award from the governor for her work.

My office was located on the fourth floor of the hotel, in the back of the sales and marketing area. I immediately had an office built for me behind the front desk in the lobby with a door that led right out to the reception front desk. I told the staff at the front desk to come and get me any time they needed me to handle a guest situation, as I never wanted them to become rude with a guest. I left that door that led from my office to the check in desk open most of the time so they knew that I meant it … and so I could hear how they were speaking with our guests.

I had a miscellaneous counter built at the end of the front desk so guests could buy things they needed 24 hours a day, such as aspirin, a shirt, a tie, magazines, a newspaper, and those sorts of things. All those years I traveled, I hated seeing the hotel shop closed when I needed something. The front desk team looked after this area. Although this is common in hotels today, it wasn't back then.

I had a Resident Manager (#2 position in a hotel), Doreen Robinson. She worked days just as I did, so I had a lot of issues and problems on the night shift.

Most guests arrived from 4:00pm on, and I needed mature, experienced leadership on the night shift. There aren't too many problems that occur between 9:00am and 5:00pm in a business hotel because the guests check out between 7:00am and 9:00am in the morning and arrive between 4:00pm and 8:00pm in the evening. That said, I made sure that I had the right leadership on at the right times. Ultimately this was the very reason why I arrived at 6:00am, before my guests woke up.

I told Doreen that she had to begin working from 3:00pm until 1:00am. I would be the day general manager, and she would be the evening general manager. I am not sure she appreciated my humor on this subject. She had worked days for her entire career, so I'm not sure she was very happy about this, but she did it well, and my problems at night went away immediately. She was a real professional.

My schedule was very routine. *I believe in routine to gain consistency and build accountability in operations.* Routine can be very boring I must admit. Peter Drucker, the management guru of the 20th century once said, "Management is boring. If you want excitement, become a race car driver."

I came in at 6:00am every morning. I first looked in all three of our public elevators to make sure they were clean, and I checked the lobby and the driveway for cleanliness. I even checked the blue U.S. Post Office mailbox on the corner to make sure it was clean. Mr. Marriott once told me to keep those mailboxes clean if they are near the hotel.

You would be surprised what you will find in elevators or in your driveway in the morning. They are usually things you don't want your guests to see. I then took an elevator up to the 14th floor and walked every floor to make sure that there were no room service trays or tables in the hallways with nasty-looking dirty dishes from the night before (I hate that). Have you ever seen a piece of prime rib on a plate at 6:00am in a hotel hallway that was served to the guest 12 hours before? It is not a pretty sight.

I also wanted to make sure that the express checkouts and newspapers had been delivered, and that the floors and stairwells were clean. When I first started this, I would find a lot of trays in the halls. After I explained my expectations to my room service team in this area, soon I did not find another tray or room service table in the halls in the morning. I think they checked at midnight and again around 5:45am before I got there in the morning. They knew that I checked every day without fail. It is amazing how when you are a good role model and set high expectations things get done, especially if you personally check up on your expectations. As they say, "Inspect what you expect."

I worked my way down to the 4th floor, arriving there at 6:15am. This is the floor that all of the banquet, convention space, and production kitchens were on. I walked all of the space as the banquet team was setting up for breakfast and meetings. I walked the front and then the back to see if everything was put away and locked up from the night before. I checked every storeroom and walked the kitchens to see if we were in good shape and ready for breakfast on time. I looked in every walk-in cooler to make sure that all of the food was dated and rotated properly and that the third shift had left the place spotless. I noted safety issues and asked the staff if they knew of any as I made my daily tours through all departments. I also thanked them for doing a great job and told them that I would see them again later that day.

I then checked the employee cafeteria for cleanliness as well as the employee locker rooms. I wanted the locker rooms to look great so that when the employees arrived at work they had clean, well maintained locker and changing rooms to get ready in. I wanted the showers and the room clean enough that I would want to use them. I remember back when I was a front-line employee the locker rooms, showers, and toilets were often disgusting. I now had the authority to fix things like that. I checked every single public restroom as well, including the ladies' restroom, as no guests were usually around that early.

After this, I worked my way down to the lobby level and checked the driveway and the lobby condition again, as our guests would soon be coming down for breakfast and checkout.

In a business hotel, the guests leave early. A general manager who comes in at 9:00am in the morning would never see any of his or her guests. I learned that different positions require different schedules.

I then headed to the restaurant to make sure the breakfast setup was going well. By now it would be 6:45am. I would then check out room service, go down to the basement to check the receiving dock and trash dumpster for cleanliness and security. I would then check in with the morning maintenance team to see what issues we had. By 7:00am, I made my way to my office with a full Day-Timer® of notes to review with my executive committee. They knew that in 24 hours I would be taking this walk again and that they needed to get their assignments accomplished before then, if I had found any issues with their departments. Safety issues were always to be fixed first and immediately.

From 7:30am–8:30am, I walked the banquet spaces again, greeting every meeting planner and assisting them in any last minute needs they had. I checked the restaurants several times and hung out in the lobby to talk with my guests and to help the staff with any difficult issues that might arise. I had no meetings scheduled before 9:00am as I wanted to be out and about with my staff and guests.

I made this tour again from 11:00am to noon. I went to the health club and worked out from 3:00pm–4:00pm, I inspected rooms from 4:00pm–5:00pm and then again from 5:00pm–6:00pm, I did my evening routine hotel tour and then I was out of there. I got home at 6:10pm, unless there was an important event in the hotel, but sometimes I just went home and came back later for those events. Living close to work made this possible. This way I got to see every employee every day on all three shifts. Everyone knew who I was and what I wanted. The third-shift cleaner told me that he had been there for 10 years, and I was the first general manager he had ever met and, for that matter, had ever seen.

I implemented checklist systems in every department and checked them as I walked around for compliance. I used these walks also to stop and show employees the right way to do something. From something as small as how to cut lemon wedges properly to how to use a knife safely; to how to lift heavy objects to how to respond better the next time with a guest situation.

I had a desk and telephone put in the lobby right in front of the check-in desk and had a nameplate made that said Lee Cockerell, General Manager. I would sit out there and do my work several hours a day so guests could talk with me, the staff could see me, and send guests over as well. This really blew them away. You do some things for effect. My staff knew I was serious about excellence.

I personally made up our mission statement. I did not ask anyone's opinion or set up a committee to study it. I made it simple so no one would forget it. "Be so nice to the guests that they can't believe it."

I told all of my employees that if they would do this, I would provide them whatever resources and training they needed to get their jobs done. I still get notes from some of them years later that end with, "Lee, don't forget to be so nice to the guests that they can't believe it." Still today, if you go back there, you will find employees who remember this and practice it. Being nice is the most important service standard you can have as my 13-year-old granddaughter Margot told me when I was writing my second book, *The Customer Rules: The 39 Essential Rules for Delivering Sensational Service.*

In the afternoon from 4:00pm–5:00pm, I inspected 30 rooms every day. I did what I called a one-minute inspection. This was walking into the room and seeing how it felt, looked, and smelled. I wore a little apron that had pockets in it where I kept extra bars of soap, shampoo, and a rag.

If a bar of soap was missing, I replaced it; and if the mirror had a spot on it, I wiped it. I wrote that in my Day-Timer® and when I was finished, I discussed it with the housekeeper who had cleaned that room and later with the executive housekeeper. This way I got a look at every room in the hotel, every eight to nine days. The one thing I told the housekeepers that I needed from them was no hair in the bathrooms. Hair in a bathroom, especially when it is not yours, is a major problem. They thought that was funny, but they remembered it. Every time I saw a housekeeper I would say, "No hair." After a while when they saw me they would say, "No hair," even if they did not speak English. I told them I could handle a little dust on the picture frames, but no hair!

I added a full-size ironing board and an iron to every room, plus a coffee maker and a dish of hard candy. I put a note on the dresser that said, "If you need anything or if anything is wrong, let me know"; and I signed it, Lee Cockerell, General Manager. This is what I mean when I say there are ways to put pressure on yourself to force you to be a better manager and leader.

I put a round gold sticker on all of the restaurant menus that said, "If you have any problems that the restaurant manager can't or won't resolve, call me 24 hours a day. The operator and the restaurant manager have my home phone number." You know I never received a call. I wonder why? The service immediately improved in the restaurant the day these stickers went on the menus.

The reason I was able to be a great general manager, even though I had never done it before, was that I had traveled for almost 10 years. I had checked into and out of more hotel rooms than I even want to think about. I have stayed in and used the services of the best hotels in the world as a guest. I knew what was important from a guest's perspective, and that is what I focused on. No hair in the bathroom was at the top of my list.

- I opened the health club/exercise room 24 hours a day, as my travels had taught me that many people need to get in there early or late. Common today but not back then.

- I built that miscellaneous counter into the end of the desk so guests could get the things they needed 24 hours a day. Common today but not back then.

- I put an express breakfast buffet in place to speed up service, as business guests are always in a hurry.

- I put coffee in the rooms because that is main thing in the lives of business travelers. Common today but not back then.

- I put the full-size ironing boards and irons in the rooms because ironing on one of those miniature boards is ridiculous, and waiting for them to be delivered is painful. Pretty common today but not back then.

I put up signs in all of the back-of-the-house areas that read: *"SAFETY: If a safety issue exists that your manager is not fixing, or if you have any concerns about a safe work environment that your manager is not addressing, call me 24 hours a day. The operator has my home phone number and will get me on the line. Lee Cockerell, General Manager, Extension 5434."*

Again I never got a call. The managers learned to take care of these things and to pay attention to employee concerns, ideas, and suggestions. I put in place total expectations and total accountability. I got really focused on this safety issue because my bonus was hit really hard the first year I was there due to high-accident frequency.

We started a stretching program for all of the housekeepers every morning to cut down on back strains. We made it a policy that housekeepers were not allowed to turn a mattress alone. We made sure they wore eye protection when they sprayed chemicals.

In food and beverage, I had a good heart-to-heart talk with my executive chef and told him that the kitchen floors were always to be dry and needed to figure out how to make that happen. Also, all food-preparation employees were required to wear a protective glove when they were using a knife. I went through every department and put these procedures and safety rules in place, and my accident frequency plummeted:

- If the floors are dry, you don't fall.
- If you have the glove on (including management to set a good example), you don't have cuts.
- If you stretch, you have fewer back injuries and so on.

Everyone who had an accident had to come and see me

with his or her manager and explain what happened. What was on the accident report was often quite different than what the employee told me. I was looking for the real causes, so I could put in operating guidelines and training to avoid the same thing again. I needed to know the real reason the accident happened.

I interrogated the employee the way Judge Judy does to learn the truth. If someone was out of work with a lost-time accident, we visited him or her at home and kept closely in touch so each employee knew we cared and that we missed each one of them and wanted him or her back to work. I personally called each employee frequently at home to see how he or she was coming along.

The hotel was so small that I was able to be everywhere. One thing that I learned for sure is that what is important to the general manager of a hotel is what is important to the staff. I guarantee you that the general manager is the most important person in any organization, not the corporate folks.

This was the best job that I had ever had up to this point in my career. I was able to make a difference every day for my guests and staff, unlike being in a bureaucratic, headquarters office.

I set up an advisory group of front-line employees and met with them every Thursday for an hour. They were from every department. In addition, I had my director of human resources and director of maintenance in the room, as most of the problems the employees brought up related to these two areas.

My secretary, Angie Rowe, took down everything that

every employee told me about, from a leaky faucet that needed repairing to equipment shortages; from safety issues to a broken vacuum cleaner. We sent that list to the department heads every week so they could fix the issues hopefully before the next Thursday. Angie was very organized and followed up on everything for me. The lesson? If you have a secretary or an administrative assistant, make sure they are highly organized with strong administrative skills.

The following Thursday we went over each item to see if it was completed. Every item was chronologically numbered and stayed on the list until resolved. We posted that list on all of the bulletin boards so the employees could see that I was listening to them and getting things accomplished. I was removing the hassles from their jobs so they could perform at the highest level and in turn this removed hassles from our guests.

This is the power of routine and process. The more issues I took care of, the more my associates told me. I learned the value of involving the staff in their work. I learned that this builds high trust. This process made sure that nothing was forgotten or slipped through the cracks.

If someone brings something to your attention and you don't follow up, your credibility falls to zero. It is easy to believe that an issue is a small thing and unimportant to follow up on. What I learned however was that while it may be a small issue to me, it often was a big, important issue for the person bringing it to my attention. I wanted to have 100% credibility with 100% of our staff.

I learned that you have to communicate and market to your

associates what you have done for them. If I did something for my team, I let them know what I did.

One day within the first week I was in Springfield, I walked into the Grand Ballroom and noticed there was a cigarette burn in the tablecloth of one of the banquet tables. This was a lunch for 300 guests, and the doors were going to open in a few minutes. I told Sharon, the banquet captain, to change the tablecloth. She looked at me like I was crazy. She said, "I will just put the salt and pepper shaker over the burn hole." I said, "No, change it." She said, "But we are about to open the doors." I said, "Then, you better hurry." She did not realize that I knew a lot about the banquet department, as that's where I got my start. I think that morning she thought I was a nut. Ten years later I received a letter from her while at Disney. I had of course long forgotten this incident.

She said in her letter to me that she wanted to thank me for setting such an example of excellence and attention to detail back in Springfield. She recounted the cigarette burn story to me and said that that encounter with me had changed the way she thought about her management responsibilities and personal as well as professional standards and that she believes this is the main reason she is so successful today.

Don't ever forget that if you are going to be excellent, everything matters. Attention to detail is the name of the game for excellence in all things. All leaders are made up of their experiences in life and whom they have worked for and with. This was what had happened to Sharon that morning. Never underestimate the impact you can have on someone.

Boy, I love to hear those stories. That's where the big satisfaction and payoff comes from being a leader. It's like your children telling you when they grow up how much they appreciate the way you raised them, even though there were moments along the way when they didn't care much for your parental direction.

The one thing I always did was to make sure that the front-line employees knew that leadership was available when they needed us and if a guest situation was too difficult, they were to stay polite and professional and get a leader, whether that leader was in a meeting or not. The guests came first, as did supporting the front-line cast. My policy was to never tell a guest that a manager was in a meeting if that guest had an issue and asks to see the manager. There is seldom, or ever, a meeting more important than a customer.

During a major renovation of the hotel in Springfield, we had to close the lobby for months and have our guests check in on the banquet level on the fourth floor. I anticipated we were going to have some unhappy guests during this time. The restaurants would be closed too, and we would have temporary restaurants set up in banquet rooms. Knowing this, I did not want my front desk staff to get worked over by the guests day after day, then get rude and become unprofessional so I made sure that we had a table set up next to the temporary front desk. We had a manager there from 6:00am–9:00am and again from 4:00pm–8:00pm to handle difficult guest issues on the spot. At other times, a manager was paged to come. I was one of the managers who took duty at that table often.

One directive I gave was that we should hire anyone who applied for a job who had previously worked for Disney. We had great success doing this, and every one of them turned out to be great. I knew Disney's selection process was excellent and their training, even better. Hiring staff from well-respected organizations like Hilton, Marriott, Disney, Apple, Google, etc. will pay off in your career.

This general manager's position was so great because it gave me an opportunity to try out all of the management and leadership concepts I had learned over the last few years. It gave me experience working in the community, and it gave me a chance to learn more about our guests as many of them stayed with us every week. One of the greatest things though was it gave me a chance to see how great of a leader I could become.

I learned the challenge of having to worry about and balance guest satisfaction, staff attitudes and performance, morale, and business results. This was quite different than being in a staff role and much more satisfying as well.

When I left Springfield in July 1990 to join Disney, the normal management going-away party was thrown and it was nice. The thing that really made my day though was that the front-line employees took up a collection, rented the Veterans of Foreign Wars Hall in Springfield and threw an additional party for Priscilla and me, giving both of us very nice plaques with some really nice words on them about how much they appreciated our leadership, great example, and friendship.

When the front-line employees do that, you know that you have been a great leader for them. They had spent their own money on this party for us. That had never happened to me before … or since for that matter.

Our family had been through a lot of difficult things from 1988 to 1990. My mother was diagnosed with lung cancer and died along with my grandmother and idol, four months later. While we were at her funeral, Priscilla's dad stepped out of his car in Annapolis and was struck by a car. He ended up in Bethesda Naval Hospital for months and my brother had bypass surgery.

One thing that I know for sure is that if you smoke, STOP! My mother always said she could never stop smoking. She tried many times to stop. The day the doctor told her she had lung cancer she stopped, but it was too late. If not for cigarettes, she would be here probably be here today and she would know her three great-grandchildren, and they would know her. If you won't stop for yourself, then stop for your family and friends. Don't let a little piece of paper wrapped around a plant be stronger than you are.

By June 1990 everyone in our family was either gone or recovering, so Priscilla and I were ready to do something new. The hotel was running great. We had completed a $12 million renovation. I had a great team. The challenge was over. I was getting bored again.

Priscilla's life was looking up too. I bought my old company car and gave it to her when I received a new company car when we moved to Springfield. Priscilla now had the newest car she has ever had, and it was 3 years old. After driving the VW Bugs for years and that old lemon of a Chrysler that her dad had given her, she was pretty happy with this 3-year-old car. She considered it brand new.

It was now June 1990 and I had been working for 25 years (20+ to go). I am completing my 19th job. I am 45-years-old, have been married for 22 years, and Daniel is in his third year at Boston University.

I told you that when I left Marriott Corporate Headquarters in 1988 as a vice president to go to Springfield to this tiny hotel as a general manager it would turn out to be the best decision of my life. In Chapter 7, I will tell you why. That career roller coaster is moving and grooving. This time Priscilla and I are laughing from being just a little nervous, but we are very happy and excited about our next adventure. This will be our ninth relocation in 22 years! *I figure by now I have accumulated $7 million in experience, and it is starting to pay off.* Experience, I have learned, is really like money in the bank in its own unique way. "Be so nice to your guests that they can't believe it" and you will be rewarded with great business results.

7

FRANCE
1990–1993

I HAD LEARNED that there was life after dropping out of college … there was life after the Army … there was life after Hilton … there was life after getting fired … there was life after being passed over for an expected promotion … and I was about to learn there was life after Marriott.

Almost all people survive the thrill of a ride on the *Big Career Roller Coaster* as long as they stay seated, keep their seatbelts fastened, stay professional, stay positive, just go with the flow, and have fun! When it stops, get off and get refocused for the next ride. The other word for this is LIFE!

It was June 1990, and I was really enjoying my life as a general manager in Springfield. The place had been totally renovated. The hotel is running perfectly. I have a great team. I was

175

able to come and go as I please. I made 99% of the decisions about the hotel without checking with anyone. I may not be a vice president now, but I'm a "big deal" in the Springfield Marriott. As a vice president in Washington, D.C., I was a small fish in a big pond; in Springfield, I was a big fish in a small pond. Life was good in the pond.

What More Could One Want?

Well, one day the phone rang. It was a Disney executive, Sanjay Varma, who was responsible for opening the then Euro Disney Resort, which today is Disneyland® Paris. I had worked with him years before at Marriott. At one point he reported to me at Marriott, and then we were peers. He had left Marriott a couple of years before to join Disney and now he had a position he wanted me to take at Disney in Paris, reporting to him.

This is going to happen to many of you in your professional careers, so *be respectful and nice to everyone on the way up, as you never know who will be your boss one day.* It may well be someone who reported to you a long time ago, and they will remember the real you. Direct reports often have a different opinion of you than your peers and your boss.

The position Sanjay was offering to me was director of food and beverage and quality assurance for the Euro Disney Resort. He told me the project was scheduled to open on April 12, 1992, which was 2 years away.

I was thinking, "I had been in food and beverage for 23 years before I became a general manager. Why would I want to do this?"

I clearly understood why he wanted me to take this position. Food and beverage is what I had the most expertise in— and that is what he needed! He needed someone who could organize the food and beverage operations. He wanted someone who was good at organizing big projects, and that's what I'm good at.

My hotel in Springfield was running smoothly. We had done a $12 million renovation of this 250-room hotel. The place looked great.

Marriott loved me again, and it would not be long before they would give me a bigger hotel to run. I had a great salary; a company car, a great healthcare plan, stock options and I lived eight minutes from work. Daniel was only 90 minutes away at Boston University, and we saw him frequently at his rugby games and other times as well. Life was almost perfect.

These were all perks. The only anti-perk was that I was bored to death now that the hotel was running so well. There weren't really any challenges left. I work better when things are a mess and when there are lots of challenges. I seem to thrive in chaotic situations. Why in the world would I give up an almost perfect life for a high-risk life and even consider starting over with another company just because of being bored? The answer to that question is simple; boredom is mentally painful and will affect your performance and health over time.

I went home that night and told Priscilla about the offer from Disney. I said, "Disney has a position in Paris at Euro Disney for me, and they want me to go to Orlando Tuesday for an interview with several Disney executives. What do you think?" You can see that I have matured, since I am asking Priscilla's opinion versus back in Los Angeles 17 years ago when I took that job in Lancaster against her better judgment and advice ... and promptly got fired 90 days later.

I expected her to say, "No! Lee, things are good here and why take a chance? You have been with Marriott for 17 years, and we have a good life."

What she did say was, "Yes! Let's go." I was shocked at her quick response. I said, "Why?" She said, and I will never forget her exact words, "Lee, we get to live in Paris, this is Disney, and they are going to pay you. If you don't do this, you will look back in 5 years and have regrets!"

I said, "Okay." We literally made the decision in five minutes. The next morning I booked the trip to Orlando, flew down and had the round of interviews and made the deal.

This was the first time I had ever been to the Walt Disney World® Resort. Somehow we had never brought Daniel to Disney World. He has finally forgiven us. We did take him to Disneyland® in Anaheim when I worked in Los Angeles at the Hilton. Disneyland was so much fun, and he was only two. After the first time we took him, the next few times we left him with a babysitter and just Priscilla and I went. We did not tell him where we were going.

It's funny looking back how things worked out for me in going to Disney. In June 1989, just one year before, Daniel called me at work in Springfield. He was on the Walt Disney World® College Program for the summer. He worked at the front desk of Disney's Contemporary Resort. He said, "Hi,

Dad. I have some bad news for you. Disney is better than Marriott!" You see he had worked at the Copley Marriott Hotel for a year during his freshman year at Boston University. I said, "Why do you say that?" He said, "Because the training is really great. It is much better than Marriott training."

That statement surprised me, as I thought we did a great job of training our associates at Marriott, but the vote was in from someone who had experienced both. The lesson here is that you are never as good as *you* think you are, you can always be better and it is never too late to learn from others and it is never too late to get better.

I was scheduled to go to a Marriott Regional Management meeting with my boss and several other Marriott general managers from our region on Thursday, and here I was in Orlando interviewing. I received a call Tuesday afternoon from my secretary. She told me that the Marriott Hotel in Boston where we were supposed to have the meeting on Thursday had experienced a bad fire and that the meeting was now going to be in my hotel in Springfield, and that I needed to get back right away to work out all of the logistics with my staff.

I hopped on a plane and got back to Springfield that evening. The meeting started Thursday morning. I called my boss, Colin Nadeau and told him I needed to meet with him for coffee before the meeting started. We met, and I resigned. I needed to do this, as I could never get through a three-day meeting knowing I was leaving. I wanted to be the one to tell him and not have the grapevine get to him first. He had been a good leader for me and I highly respected him.

The second thought I had was, "What have I done? Why do I keep doing these things? I don't speak French. I have never lived in Europe. Why do I keep taking these risks?" There were a million other thoughts too. I didn't sleep well for the next few nights as I came to grips with what we were about to do.

This was the biggest news that had hit Springfield in years. It was like I was one of the first astronauts and that I was about to take the first rocket to the moon. My departure to Disney was front-page news in Springfield. The lesson here is never forget how powerful the name Disney is in the world and how respected it is for being the best. I was not the one who had created the interest. It was Disney. If I had been leaving for another hotel company, it would have been on page 4 of the business section instead of the front page.

I may have not been sleeping well, but Priscilla was sleeping like a baby and she was happy as a clam after my resignation from Marriott. She was dreaming of living in Paris, which was a dream of hers many years before. I was sleeping like a baby too—I woke up every two hours and cried.

I forgot to tell you earlier in this series what Priscilla said to me back in 1966 when I first met her and tried to get her to go out with me on a date. She was 19 and was the secretary to the director of food and beverage at the Washington Hilton Hotel. I was 21 and a clerk in the food and beverage control office next door. She often came into my office to use our pencil sharpener, which was screwed to the metal file cabinet.

I finally asked her out, and she said, "No!" She offered no alternative and no hope. She told me she had a French boyfriend and some day she planned to live in France and that her children would speak French and English.

This all turned out to be true 24 years later in 1990, but it was with me and not with him. I love this story. Today everyone in our family speaks French but me.

I waited a few weeks and said, "Priscilla, what about just going for an early daylight dinner?" She said, "No." I thought the word daylight would disarm her, but it didn't change her mind.

A few more months went by and I said, "Priscilla, what about just going out for a drink?" She said, "No." This woman was getting on my nerves, as I am not used to people saying "No" to me.

About a year had passed by now and I said one day, "Priscilla, what about lunch? That is all I want. No strings attached. Just lunch. After all we work right next door to each other. What is the harm in a nice lunch?"

She said that she thought I had a bad attitude and that she knew I wanted more than just lunch. She said the big "no" word again. I must admit I was thinking that I was going to lose this one. She had never even said the word "maybe." Later you will see that "maybe" might mean "yes."

I kept asking her, and one day she finally agreed to go to lunch … and that was the beginning of the end for her French boyfriend. Her French boyfriend already had an unfair advantage over me to begin with because he was French, and he had a red sports car that he let her drive.

I had a 1963 red Pontiac Bonneville convertible with white

leather upholstery that my mother had given me. It was great, but that little red sports car that he had was too much competition for me. I traded in the Bonneville for a new, green two-seater Karmann Ghia (made by Volkswagen). It looked like a sports car, but it did not have the style and power of her boyfriend's car—but it was all I could afford. I financed that car at 4% interest and paid $2,000 for it brand new. Inflation is real.

Well, today Priscilla has lived in France with me for 3 years from 1990 to 1993. Daniel has married a French woman, Valerie, and her grandchildren speak French, so it all worked out just fine. It worked just as she had predicted back in 1966 when she told me that she would live in France and her children would speak French and English.

Now you know why Priscilla said, "yes" so fast when I asked, "Should we take this job in Paris with Disney?" Now you know the rest of the story. Living in Paris was a dream come true for her.

Right about now you are probably thinking to yourself or saying to a friend or coworker, "Why is Lee telling us about his pursuit of Priscilla? What does that have to do with career development?"

What it has to do with career development is the same thing it has to do with life: *If you want something, don't take, "no" for an answer.* Remember, I still had breakfast and brunch and church and many other things I could ask her out for that she hadn't said "no" to yet. *Patience is a virtue for sure, and persistence is often what gets you what you want.*

A friend of mine, Ben May, is a real salesman. He said the fun starts when the client says, "No." That is when the challenge begins. "NO" does not always mean, "No!" Sometimes it means not right now. I think far too many people give up too soon on what they want when they get a little resistance. Don't mistake obstacles for anything other than a detour. Detours take a little longer but you still arrive at your destination.

We put our house in Springfield on the market. The housing market was terrible. We had hardly any prospective buyers. I called the man who was going to replace me as general manager and told him that I thought he would love my house.

He and his wife looked at it and told me that they thought it was too dark inside and that they wanted a house with more light. It actually was a cloudy day, and the house was dark inside when they visited. I convinced him and his wife to come back on a bright, sunny day; we had every light on in the house. They said that they liked it, but could not afford it.

Now we are talking about a bear market in housing in New England in June 1990. Of course, it was a bull market when we bought the house 2 years before. We like to buy high and sell low it seems.

I asked him what he could afford. He told me what they could pay. I said, "That is exactly the price I need." We lost $18,000 on that house after only living in it for 2 years, but my theory is to cut your losses and move on. That house 2 years later was down another $20,000. As the old saying goes, "It could be worse."

Up until that time I didn't know another person who has

had to take a check to closing, no one that will admit it anyway. Moving often and buying houses can be a big anti-perk. Doing it all over today I would rent for certain assignments.

I accepted the job with Disney at an even lower salary than what I was making as general manager of the Springfield Marriott. An adventure like this has value, plus Priscilla might have done something bad to me if I had not taken the job over a matter of a few thousand dollars. There were some other perks that made up for the loss of base salary. It was a fair deal because the perks and anti-perks balanced each other out! I was able to negotiate more stock options in lieu of a higher salary and that turned out really well.

I departed for the Walt Disney World® Resort for six weeks of training on July 8, 1990, after doing a 30-day turnover with my successor in Springfield. This is way too long for the turnover, but I had such good relationships with the community and the employees that my boss asked me to stay that long. At the end of a couple of weeks, the new general manager wanted me gone … and I wanted to be gone. I acted interested in the job in Springfield those last 30 days, but it was pure acting. My heart and mind were at Disney, and I was ready to get to Paris.

I had a whirlwind kind of training in Orlando. By the end of the six weeks, my head was spinning. I was dreaming about CRs, CTs, cannibalization, and a million other terms that I had no idea what these people at Walt Disney World were talking about. My biggest challenge was to try to get from one trailer to another to meet whoever was training me. It seemed like everyone was in a trailer. This seemed quite odd to me at the time. No one can explain to you how things really work at the Walt Disney World® Resort. You have to work there for a long time to figure it all out, but one thing is for sure ... it works! Many departments were in trailers because the resort had expanded so fast they couldn't build offices fast enough.

I remember how some people presumed the strangest things. I was talking to someone one day during my training and at the end of the session she said, "Lee, your English is very good." I said, "Thank you." I did not want to say to her, "I hope so since I am American, and it is the only language I speak." I think she presumed that since I was going to Euro Disney that I must be French. I found this very funny! The lesson here is, be careful about what you assume.

It rained every afternoon in July and August in Orlando, so hard that I could not believe it. I hope that comes back soon, as every few years we end up in a drought. Wouldn't it be interesting if when we were born an instruction book came along with us, and it laid out exactly what was going to happen to us in our lives right down to the day we were going to die?

I don't think so. While that system would make things much clearer, life would not be very exciting and depending on the playbook, it might be downright discouraging. Many people achieve far more than they think they are capable of with nothing more than pure determination. Don't put limits on your dreams and don't let anyone tell you what you can or can't do. Write your own playbook and make it full of high expectations for yourself.

Priscilla flew down to Orlando from Springfield for our

22nd wedding anniversary on August 3, 1990, and we celebrated it at the Chefs de France restaurant at Epcot®. The next week, I hired the chef of that restaurant for Euro Disney. The Chefs de France Restaurant just added another chapter to our family history. The summer of 2014, our grandson Jullian worked there as a waiter and loved it. He was born in Paris and speaks fluent French, so he was the perfect candidate to be hired. I really believe everyone should be a waiter or waitress at some time in life. This experience teaches you a lot. I was a waiter in several places, Daniel was a waiter at Phillip's Crab House in Ocean City, Maryland and now Jullian is a waiter. Margot and Tristan are next when they are old enough. This position teaches you how to be organized, move quickly, stay composed under pressure and generally, how to engage with all kinds of people.

I flew to Paris in early September, more or less trained in the "Disney Way." This was hard—let me tell you! My head was still spinning.

I arrived in Paris on a Sunday morning. I was supposed to be picked up at Charles de Gaulle Airport by the vice president of Euro Disney.

I was not totally unfamiliar with France, as we had visited there often through the years with our friends, Suzie and Alain Piallat, so I wasn't uncomfortable or unaware of the city or the culture. I will tell you a short story about one of my past experiences in France before I tell you the rest of the airport, pickup story on that Sunday morning.

The other times on our visits to France, Priscilla had been

with me and she speaks French. Actually one year we had gone to France in the summer and arrived on June 21 to an all-night music festival called, Fête de Musique. Hundreds of musical groups play all over France from rooftops to sidewalks. It is quite a *"magical"* experience. Our friends, Alain and Suzie, could not go to Paris that year, so it was arranged for us to stay with Alain's father, Pascal, in his apartment in the Latin Quarter on the left bank in Paris. He was a treat to stay with and made sure that we saw the best of Paris. Pascal always made sure we had good food and wine when we stayed with him. He bought special wine for us and would not let us drink his, ordinary wine as he called it. He even bought a can of corn and put it in the salad one night because he had heard that all Americans love corn. In France back then corn was pretty much used only to feed the farm animals. Pascal would go out every day and buy a morning baguette for lunch and then go back and buy a fresh afternoon baguette for dinner. Food was and is a big deal and important in France, and I am glad that it is because we were the winners.

Pascal had attended hotel school with two other gentlemen 50 years before, and they each owned a hotel in the village of Dijon in the Burgundy wine region. Of course, this is the town that made Dijon mustard famous as well. One morning he and his friends, including Priscilla, Daniel, and I, drove to Dijon and had lunch at one of his old friends' hotels.

We were a party of twelve. I remember at the end of that meal they brought out a cheese trolley that had at least 40 different cheeses on it. This was way beyond what we had back in

Oklahoma with the basic Velveeta, Swiss, Cheddar, and American cheese. Brie did not even get to Oklahoma until long after I was gone, and even then, Americans heated it up in the oven and had it as a hors d'oeuvre. It was a spectacular lunch in a beautiful hotel restaurant in a quaint village, memorable at the least. Priscilla was in heaven, as she adores all cheeses.

After lunch we all drove out into the Burgundy wine country and stopped at a couple of vineyards where the entire French contingent had a lot of conversation with the local owners. After a couple of stops, we had still not been offered any wine to taste, and I wasn't really sure what was going on as I didn't understand a word of French. At one stop, one of the ladies in the wine cellar spoke English. I asked her, what were the best recent vintages of wine in Burgundy? She told me that the 1976 and 1978 were superb, the best in several years. This small bit of information would save my life or at least my self-respect within the hour, proving once again the value of asking questions.

We went to the next vineyard, as they are right next door to one another for kilometer after kilometer. The vineyards are narrow and run up the sloping hills. It is absolutely a beautiful site. When we arrived at the next vineyard and got out of our cars, we were greeted by this tanned, handsome Frenchman. It took between three and four minutes for all of the greetings and kissing to take place. If you are a regular friend, you get kissed once on each cheek and you have to kiss everyone else on the cheeks as well … and if you are a really special friend, the kisses move to three for each person. I think there is a category for four kisses, but I never learned what that was. I like this tradition, and it is one we have adopted in our family since we now can claim French relatives.

The first thing our host did was to ask our son Daniel what he would like to drink. He said a Coke, of course. They did not have Coke but served him a Pepsi of all things. He was happy. When you are twelve, you don't need much to make you happy. He had already survived a French lunch earlier in the day. He was not offered a children's menu and, therefore, got no macaroni and cheese, hot dogs, or chicken fingers. These were the years before McDonalds® had come to France. Today most kids in France want to go to McDonalds® just as they do here in the United States.

We all proceeded into a small wine cellar with gravel on the floor and a few very large wooden barrels of wine stacked around the room. The cellar was dark and only lighted by one single light bulb hanging from the ceiling. Everyone was talking and having a grand time. The owner let each of us try a sip of the wine that was fermenting in the large wooden casks to see how it was progressing. Suddenly there was a roar of laughter from the French group. They had been talking together and, of course, I had no clue what they were talking about. I learned in a minute that they had told the owner that I was an American hotelman and a food and beverage expert.

He said something to the group in French, and they were all staring at me with semi-serious smiles on their faces. I said to our friend Pascal, "What did he say?" He told me that our host had said, "So let's see how much the American hotelman knows about wine." I was at that moment wishing that I had some arsenic pills that I could crush between my teeth, but I did not, so I smiled and acted as if this were no big deal.

Our host went into the back and brought out the largest Burgundy wine glasses I had ever seen. They each looked like they would hold a full bottle or two of wine. He then returned to the back and brought out a dusty bottle of red Burgundy wine. There are white Burgundies too, by the way. He handled the bottle in a very gentle and careful way, like a newborn baby. He wiped it and cleaned it up before taking his corkscrew and opening it. He then looked at me with what I perceived as a wicked smile, but I could have been wrong since I was in the middle of a nervous breakdown. I could hear my heart beating and was glad that I knew that they couldn't hear it.

You see here are my wife and my son watching. I am thinking that I am about to be humiliated in front of nine Frenchmen who knew more about wine when they were in the first grade than I do now. The worst part is that my son is going to see me humiliated in front of all of these people. He thinks I know everything. Priscilla does not bother me as much as she knows that I don't know everything.

He gently poured about two ounces of wine in one of the gigantic glasses and handed it to me. I took it and held it up to the light and swirled it around for about 15 seconds. I acted as if I were studying it carefully for the heaviness of the wine as it slipped down the glass in a wave-like motion. This is called "ropes." I had learned this back in my wine class at the Waldorf Astoria 10 years before. The slower the wine drifts down the glass, the more body it has. I said, "Good ropes." Our French friend translates, and there is a glimmer of respect from the faces of all of the onlookers. It is very quiet as I bring the glass to my nose while continuing to swirl it around to check the aroma. It smelled quite good. I said, "Good nose."

I took what seemed like a long time and looked at the wine again and then put a small amount in my mouth and sucked it over my tongue just like we had learned in class. I swirled it in my mouth while looking up, as if I were contemplating what vintage this wine was. Of course, I have no idea but I do know it is a very good wine. I had learned to tell the difference between great wines and mediocre wines, and I was sure that by the way he handled the wine he was not serving me something that was not special.

I took a few more seconds and took one more taste and then said, "This is a '78 Burgundy; no wait, this is a '76 Burgundy." Our host immediately in an excited voice said, "Voila!" … which kind of means, "you got it." In a flash, everyone in the room was congratulating me with handshakes and kisses. I saw the look of pride on Daniel's face and the look of disbelief on Priscilla's face. I had done it. It was a great guess!

I did not tell Priscilla and Daniel the truth until we got home three weeks later, as I wanted to savor my new fame. I told them though it was a good guess and how I had used the information the lady had given me about the recent great vintages. It was a calculated guess I suppose you could say.

This left a lasting impression on my son; and in the 12th grade, he wrote an essay on how his dad had saved the pride of America in France. He starts the essay with the notion that most French people think that Americans only know about McDonalds® and Coca-Cola® and his dad proved them wrong on that bright, sunny day in Burgundy. In his essay I was an American hero.

I learned that if you keep calm and cool and think, then you can guess the truth—or get really close by just taking your time and asking question along the way. They would have been impressed if I had stuck with my first guess of 1978. For all I knew, it was an 1878 or a 1962 wine, but the lady in the wine cellar with whom I spoke told me about the best vintages. *The real lesson here is that when you ask questions and then take the time to listen to people and respect their thoughts and perspective, these learnings can be a springboard to success.*

All of my previous trips to France and experiences over the years, like this wine tasting did make a big difference in my comfort level that Sunday morning arriving at the airport. The HR department in Orlando had faxed my flight number and my picture to the person responsible for picking me up

Do you know what a faxed photo looks like? It looks like a gray, black, and white blob. It could have been the picture of anything you can imagine, so the person picking me up could not spot me. Finally we did get together, and he dropped me at my temporary apartment. Priscilla is not coming for two weeks, so I am alone until then.

He gave me the keys to my company car and a map to the office for the next morning, and he leaves me. I am exhausted not only from the flight, but from the stress of what I was about to get into. I now live in France. That is a sudden and scary thought. I am alone, and I don't speak French. I take a nap. Sleep and hot water are the two big healers in my opinion for physical and mental pain.

When I woke up about 4:00pm, I was hungry so I walked down to the Avenue de Vincennes, which is a large boulevard. There are cafes and stores everywhere, but you don't understand how intimidated I am of the French ... and I don't speak a word of French! I could hardly say, "Bonjour!" Actually I could say it, but I was afraid if I did, they might think I spoke French and then what would I do when they said a bunch of other French words back to me. Better to just keep quiet, I decided.

I went into a shop that had a sandwich case. I spotted a ham-and-cheese sandwich. I actually did know what Jambon (ham) was, and I knew what Fromage (cheese) was. I ran those two words through my mind a couple of times and finally said, "Madame, Jambon et Fromage, s'il vous plaît." I was happy when she smiled and gave me that sandwich. I said, "Merci." I at least knew nine French words, I found out. This was a big deal. I had done it. I was not going to starve before Priscilla arrived.

I gave the store clerk 20 francs and hoped that she gave me the correct change. I was wondering, "What were all of these coins worth?" It wasn't long before I could order a beer, a wine, a coffee, and so on. I soon discovered that I actually knew more French words than I thought I did. Remember, croissant—this is a very good word for breakfast. My variety expanded after about two weeks of Jambon et Fromage sandwiches. By the time I left France I still could not speak French, but I knew a lot of French words; and I got by as I was no longer intimidated.

It is amazing how you can be afraid of something and then before long be totally comfortable with it. *The lesson here is don't ever underestimate what you can do if you put your mind to it or even if you are thrown into it. Everything is hard before it is easy but when you do the hard things life gets easier and more exciting.*

One thing I love about all of the cities I have lived in is that I know my way around those cities. I feel at home in all of them even today. I was driving like a Frenchman within a couple of weeks and could find my way into and out of Paris without any problem at all.

The good thing about France is that the French people don't carry on small talk with you in the stores and cafes the way Americans do. You order your coffee. They give you your coffee. You ask for the check. They give you the check. They don't ask where you are from or tell you a joke or anything else and that was just fine with me because I did not want to talk with them, I couldn't! Coming to the United States and not speaking English must be a nightmare because here anybody and everybody is trying to talk to you about this or that.

I went off to work on Monday morning, leaving really early just in case. The office was supposedly just 15 minutes away, but I am in France; and this is the first day on the job, so I am not taking any chances. The map works, and I am at work an hour early. No one else is there. I soon learn that if you want a coffee you need a two-franc coin to get it out of a machine. Nothing is free at work in France, and this is not your Maxwell House. We are talking high-test stuff here.

The days were very stressful in the beginning. Everything was different. Making a phone call seems hard. I would call some place, and the person who answered did not speak English, and I don't speak French. What do I do now? What I promptly did was get a secretary who spoke both French and English. Her name was Susan Defosse. She was from the United Kingdom, and she was great. She had my same sarcastic sense of humor so we got along, "jolly" well.

Priscilla arrived and found us an apartment on the east side of Paris, which was 25 minutes from work for me. It was a very small 1,000-square-foot apartment. There were no closets in the bedrooms, so we converted one of the bedrooms into a closet. The apartment was in a great location right next to a beautiful park and next to the Château de Vincennes, which was a Château that took up two square blocks and had a huge moat around it. It took from the early 1200s to the early 1800s to complete the construction of it … *and you thought that some of your projects take a long time to complete!*

After it was built, the king didn't really like it so he used it only as a hunting lodge when hunting in the nearby woods (the Bois de Vincennes). The king then built the palace of Versailles on the west side of Paris, which was far nicer. It was quite neat living next to this beautiful château. I thought it was terrific and loved it whether the king liked it or not. If you are ever in Paris, it is worth the time to go see it. Just take the M1 Metro east to the end of the line, get off, and there it is.

One day on my day off, I was sitting on a bench near the park and near the road reading when a car stopped and one of the occupants asked me in French for directions to the zoo. I was shocked that I understood what she said and was able to tell her the directions in French. This was a big deal to me. This did not happen often by the way, so I was pretty excited. It is funny what can make you happy in life.

We had lots of friends and family visiting for the next 3 years, just as we do in Orlando now. When we lived in Springfield, we had few visitors. Was it Paris or us that they wanted to see? I always wondered!

We had house rules for visitors, which were:

- Don't complain about your feet, as we will be doing a lot of walking.
- We will exchange your money for you once; after that, you have to do it yourself.
- We will show you how to use the Metro once, and then you are on your own.
- Don't take long showers, as we don't have much hot water.
- Eat what is on your plate when we go to a restaurant, and don't make an ugly face when you learn what it is on your plate.
- Be polite and say "bonjour" to our neighbors, as we have to live here when you are gone.

The next 2 years before Euro Disney opened was a really good life. Remember we have no guests to worry about yet and no cast members either. Last but not least, no profit to worry about. Pre-opening is a sweet time.

For the first nine months, I recruited management. I traveled all over the world interviewing candidates. We hired a lot of Europeans who were living in the United States but wanted to return to Europe, especially if they could work for Disney. Many of the people I hired are still at the Walt Disney World® Resort today doing an outstanding job in various leadership roles. They are some of Disney's best people. Others are spread around the world doing great work for other organizations.

Dieter Hannig was the head of concept development for the food and beverage operations at Euro Disney in Paris when I arrived. This was the first time I met him. Little did we know that we would be working together for a long, long time at Euro Disney and then for many years at Walt Disney World. Dieter Hannig is by far one of the best food and beverage professionals in the world and is the single reason Disney World food moved from good to great. Hiring the best really pays off.

The perk in the early months for me was traveling all over the world to all kinds of places that I had never been to. I eventually hired 225 managers for the food and beverage operations.

I learned many lessons from these leaders that I hired. One lesson on persistence is that of a lady by the name of Nora Carey. She was an American who had been living in London and now wanted to work for Disney in Paris. She had lots of skills in menu planning, menu design, cooking, teaching, and many others talents, but I really had no position for her on my staff so I told her, "No." She kept trying, and I kept saying, "No."

One day in the mail comes an invitation to attend a reception at the Ritz Hotel in Paris in honor of Julia Child, the famous American food connoisseur and author. Priscilla and I R.S.V.P.'d that we would attend.

Just a side note for all of you who sometimes don't respond when an invitation says R.S.V.P.—R.S.V.P. means to *respond whether you are coming or not.* Many people seem to think it means to call if you are coming, and others think it means to call if you are not coming. Sometimes we get a call from someone saying, "We are R.S.V.P.'ing to your party."

We then say to them, "Are you coming, or are you not coming?" It is quite unprofessional and shows a lack of manners not to respond properly to an invitation you receive that says R.S.V.P. (répondez s'il vous plaît)! This in French literally means, "respond if it pleases you," but "if it pleases you" isn't meant literally. This is a much-needed lesson for many, especially when you get an invitation from your boss and don't handle it properly. It's kind of like drinking the finger bowl, using the wrong utensil or not putting your napkin in your lap. If you are unsure watch the other diners and go last.

Back to the story at the Ritz. As we are going through the receiving line, we came up to Julia Child and who is standing next to her doing the introductions but Nora Carey! Nora said, "Julia, I would like for you to meet the Director of Food and

Beverage for Euro Disney, Lee Cockerell." Julia looks down on me, as she was quite tall, and says, "Mr. Cockerell, I hope the food is going to be better here than it is in Orlando." I don't really remember what I said. I think I grunted something like, "Me too." Her point was that food is a much more serious thing in France than it is in America.

Years later Julia came to Walt Disney World after Dieter Hannig had been in charge of our food and beverage business for some time. She was at Disney World to attend the food and wine festival. When I met her she told me, "Mr. Cockerell, the food is really good here now. I take back what I said to you back in Paris a few years ago." The real point of this story is that Nora Carey found another way to get to me. We ended up hiring her to manage all of our graphic work for the resorts including doing all of the menus and a million other things, and thank goodness we did because she did a great job! We created a job for her, which turned out to be one that we really needed … and we didn't realize it until she convinced us! That is one story about persistence, and another one is in the paragraphs below.

After the managers were all hired and on their way to Paris, Priscilla and I had time to take some nice vacations in Europe and even went to India and Nepal in 1991, three days after the Gulf War started. We went with my boss and his wife, Sanjay and Hanny Varma. Sanjay is Indian so that made the trip even better. There were only about ten people on the plane because of the war. We had to fly around Iraq on our way to India. This trip was a big perk. India is a fascinating place and quite exotic. I experienced a great example of persistence in India and learned the true meaning of the word "maybe." We were walking along the Ganges River at 6:00am one morning about to take a boat ride. By now we were numb from all of the begging. The poverty is really hard to imagine. People living on the sidewalks were common. A young man approached Priscilla and tried to sell her some homemade/handmade trinkets of some kind. She tried to put him off, but he was quite insistent. She finally said just two words to him, "maybe later."

We boarded the boat and went out into the Ganges River, which is a very holy river in the Hindu religion. People return to die near this river, and cremations are done on the banks of the river all day long. We had a great trip a few miles down the river. It was quite something watching the city awaken with thousands of people up early doing laundry in the river, selling their goods, cremations in progress, cows wandering the streets, and beggars everywhere. In India you can buy beggar coins. For a dollar, you get a handful that may be worth a half-cent each. It is a system that is required, or you would be broke in a few minutes from so many people begging. I never once felt unsafe. It is their religion that helps them cope with the poverty they find themselves in. They are a wonderful people.

We got off that boat several miles down the river, and there was the young man who had approached Priscilla an hour before to buy his goods.

He had walked along the bank following our boat all the way down. He approached her and asked her to buy some of his things. She said, "No. I am not interested." He said,

"But, madam, you said, maybe later." His persistence paid off and she bought! Great lesson here! Maybe later to him meant yes. When you are in business or personal negotiations, listen carefully to every word. Also ask yourself if you are persistent enough when you want something.

Our life was really great in 1990 and up until September 1991. The real work began around October. The pace picked up, as we were just seven months away from opening and had deadline after deadline to meet.

- We had to do everything in five languages: English, French, German, Italian, and Spanish.
- There was no, "Disney Culture" in France. We were responsible for putting that famous culture of excellence, courtesy, friendliness, and attention to detail in place.
- We were having meeting after meeting from six in the morning until sometimes past midnight.

On an average day during those last seven months before opening, I would get up at 4 in the morning and get to work by 4:45am. There is zero traffic at this time. I would usually work until around 10:00pm—that is, on average, a 17-hour day. I would get home at 10:30pm and fall in bed and get up again at 4:00am. This went on for seven months, six and seven days a week. When people tell you they work 18 hours a day, be skeptical. I surprised myself. I did not know I had that kind of stamina!

I quit drinking any alcohol a year before opening. This was tough since I love wine, and I was living in France where some of the best wines in the world are produced. I needed every single ounce of energy. I did nothing but sleep and work for seven months.

I packed one or two peanut butter and jelly sandwiches each day, as I was starving by 9 or 10:00am. I would have one then and another one for my second lunch. I can guarantee you that if you make a peanut butter and jelly sandwich and wrap it in foil, even if you forget about it, it will be fine a week later. They really stay moist. I commonly found an old one in my briefcase that I had missed and ate it days later. This saves a lot of time and it's a high-energy, tasty, and healthy sandwich. They don't sell peanut butter in France, so we had friends bring it or send it to us. While at Disney World I started bringing that sandwich again. I had forgotten how good they are and how much time you save having it with you.

I kidded Priscilla when I got home one night. I said, "Did you get up today?" She said, "What do you mean?" I said, "Well, you were in bed when I left this morning, and you are in bed now." This was semi-amusing to her only once.

Priscilla was a trooper. She did her thing in Paris and never said a word about all of my hours. She had been through openings before with me and knew how they worked. She loved Paris. I think she went to a different part of Paris every day for 3 years. Shopping for just normal household goods takes a big part of the day in France; and of course, Priscilla did not have a car. Little things like just getting your dry cleaning done were different. When you pick up a suit from the cleaners, they don't give you the hanger. They take it off the hanger and fold it up—cost savings in action. You also bag your own groceries, so you usually take your own bag with you. This is forced recycling in action and labor cost reduction.

One custom we never really got used to in France was the restaurants opening at 8:00pm. We often arrived at a restaurant at 8:00pm, and the servers and cooks were still sitting in the dining room having their dinner.

Most guests did not arrive until 9:00pm or 10:00pm. Also we had to learn to trick the servers because they won't serve you coffee until after you have had your dessert. This is the custom in France. We would tell the waiter we did not want dessert and order coffee and then as soon as the coffee was served we told the waiter we changed our mind and now would like a dessert. That way we could have our coffee and dessert together. Other things we had to learn was that the server would not come over and take your order until you close the menu. This is the signal that you are ready to order. We also learned wine is served only with food. You don't order a glass of wine as a cocktail or drink before dinner. Champagne is okay any time and for any reason. That is just the way it is, whether you like it or not.

Priscilla went around our neighborhood in Vincennes and introduced me to all of the shopkeepers where she shopped and told them that I did not speak French. She would send me to the store to get things with a note that I would hand the shopkeeper like a little kid. That was weird until I got used to it. At least with this system, I brought the right cheese home.

Opening Day April 12, 1992

We were finally ready and we opened the Euro Disney Resort at 9:00am on April 12, 1992. Well, you are never as ready as you wish, so there were a lot of problems and things to fix immediately.

We did an opening-night party for 10,000 people with the help of the great task force from the Walt Disney World® Resort. This is where I first met Meg Crofton and Don Robinson and many other people for the first time. Craig Hodges and Djuan Rivers ran the bell station, which was a tent where they checked in and out 10,000 pieces of guest luggage without losing one single piece.

This opening felt like the building of the pyramids in Egypt. There were thousands of cast members around doing everything you could imagine. I had never seen anything like it. It was of mammoth proportion.

We really could not have opened without the Walt Disney World® Task Force. There were hundreds of them. It was like the landing at Normandy in World War II. This party was a sight to behold. We bought every shrimp in Europe, and every strawberry too. We poured more champagne than I have ever seen in one place. The food cost for the party exceeded $1 million.

The grand opening went perfectly and as the night ended, we were all thrilled with the great work we had done. We finally went to bed around 4:00am. We were all geared up and staffed up to take on the huge crowds that were forecasted for the summer. We were ready. We had thought of everything.

This was going to be a great summer and one of the greatest experiences of my life.

But They Never Came!

A combination of a recession in Europe and too much negative press about how busy it would be kept people away, and we were 2,000 cast members overstaffed in the resorts. All cast members were on contracts that took at least 90 days to break, and it was still costly to break them even then. This was what I called the, "summer from Hades." I don't know what heaven is like; but after this summer, I knew what the alternative was like … and I never wanted to go there again.

We were losing one million dollars a day, each and every day in Paris between the park and resorts. You cannot even imagine what the pressure is like when you are losing one million every 24 hours. We had many visits from Michael Eisner, the CEO of the Walt Disney Company, and Frank Wells, President.

These were not pleasant visits to say the least when you are losing money at this rate.

This is like being on the Titanic, except instead of water rushing in, French francs are rushing out. The conversion to the Euro has not happened yet. You know everyone is not going to get out alive (professionally speaking).

What we went through after 9/11 at Disney World from a business perspective was like child's play compared to what we had to do in France. We had a wonderful product with great hotels, a great park, great food, and we had great Cast Members. The only thing missing were the guests, and the one really important thing, the revenue! This was the most difficult job I have had in my career, including the one where I was fired many years before.

A lot of managers and executives were biting the dust or maybe I should say, jumping overboard. The pressure was overwhelming. People were quitting, resigning, getting fired, and everything else you could think of. Divorces were happening left and right. Wives were moving back to wherever they came from; the kids were crying. It was not fun. Does this paint a good picture for you of how bad things can be? Not getting a merit increase or some reduced hours would have been like a promotion compared to what we were dealing with. We reorganized sometimes twice a week. All of the preparation was of little use, as we had to immediately change many of the concepts and processes and procedures when the guests showed up and taught us what they wanted.

I had been through difficult experiences like this many times in my career, so I just stayed cool, calm, and collected, and focused on doing the best I could with what I had to work with. If you don't believe me about how tough this opening was, ask some others who were there on Task Force like Barry Jacobson, Mark Mrozinski, Carolyn Argo, Rick Allen, Val Bunting, Dave Vermeulen, Mark Mannella, Greg Wann, Barbara Higgins, or Kim Marinaccio. There are others too, but these folks can tell you how tough things can really be. They were on the same roller coaster I was. Even Pam Landwirth, the current President of Give Kids the World who worked for us back then, was there working day and night. I think we had

90,000 test-meal coupons to give out so we could practice in the restaurants before opening to the public.

In June three months after the opening, I was promoted to vice president of Euro Disney Resorts. I replaced the vice president, who had left on the last lifeboat. Hey, I had been through tough times before, so this did not feel that bad to me. It was a lot better than being fired. My responsibilities were for the operations of the six 1,000-room resorts. I don't think I would have been able to get that promotion if I had not had the experience of being a general manager of a hotel before at Marriott. That little move to Springfield a few years before paid off. *Experience eventually starts to pay you back in real money.*

We all continued on and did the best we could. The problems really never got smaller or went away, but what happens is that you can get used to any circumstances; so after a while, we had days off and went on vacation just like normal people.

We adjusted to the "new normal." Actually, there is no such thing as "new normal," as far as I am concerned. All there is, is what is ... and as a leader, you need to learn to adjust to current circumstances instead of standing around wishing, hoping, whining, and praying that things will get back to how you would like for them to be or how they used to be. The key is to put your head down and start the painful work of getting things the way you want them instead of how they are and this often takes time.

We were in this tough set of circumstances, and I just did the best I could because that is all that I could do. I learned more about myself during this opening than I think I ever had before or have since. After that experience, working at the Walt Disney World® Resort seems like heaven. I now know from opening Euro Disney that I can hold up under any pressure that comes my way.

To make matters worse, my father-in-law, Admiral Charles Payne, Priscilla's dad, died in February 1993. In his desk was a note card with the words: *"Do your best, and then forgive yourself."* This is really all any of us can do. If you are doing your best, then you have nothing to be ashamed of. It is not so much what happens to us, but how we react to what happens. Leaders have to stay cool, calm, and collected, as everyone is watching.

We flew home to attend my father-in-law's memorial service. Everyone said a lot of wonderful things about him at the memorial service, which was held at the United States Naval Academy in Annapolis, Maryland. One thing that was said at the service about him would affect our lives in a couple of weeks back in Paris. More on that in a minute.

The minister was talking about Charlie Payne's successes in his life, from being a poor boy in Arkansas, to fighting in World War II, to graduating from the Massachusetts Institute of Technology and the Naval Academy, to becoming an admiral in the United States Navy. The minister was talking about his drive and determination to go after and achieve what he wanted. The minister went on to say that Charlie had told Sunshine, his wife, on their first date when they were 16 that he was going to marry her. Sunshine said that she thought he was a nut, but 7 years later they got married. The message the minister left us all with was that Charlie Payne did not wait to take the safe or cautious route to anything. He took immediate action!

I remember back in the '60s, a Navy officer by the name of Lloyd Bucher let the North Koreans board his vessel, the *Pueblo,* off the coast of North Korea. The North Koreans had alleged that the ship was inside the 12-mile limit. I remember Charlie telling me that Bucher should never have let the North Koreans board that ship. I said, "What should he have done?" He said, "They should have fought to the death." I remember asking him when he first knew that he was willing to die for his country, and he said it was the day that he became a naval officer and swore to the Constitution of the United States of America to defend the freedom of America. He said, "Lee, you have to decide what you stand for long before an incident happens so that you will be ready to react quickly and appropriately."

This is true for all kinds of ethical issues that all leaders are faced with every day, and this is what I learned—*be ready to do the right thing!* Remember, the paper is full of stories every day that showcase examples of leaders who made the wrong choices. By the way, the *Pueblo* is the only captured U.S. Naval vessel in the history of the United States that is still held by a foreign power and not returned. It is currently a tourist attraction in North Korea.

After the memorial service, Daniel and I flew back to Paris on his birthday which we celebrated in flight while Priscilla stayed behind to help her mother, Sunshine, square away things. It was a long, overnight flight and I thought a lot about how fragile and unpredictable life is.

Daniel and I went back to work at Disneyland® Paris and one night about eight days after we got back, I was the executive on duty for the resort. When you were the executive on duty, you did it for a week and stayed in one of the hotels to be available for any emergencies 24 hours a day.

I got a call about 8:00pm from Daniel, telling me he wanted to see me. He said he was in the lobby of the hotel. I said, "Sure. Come on up." This was not normal behavior for him, so I was a little concerned about what he was coming to tell me.

He walked in that door, not really sure what was about to happen but I already could feel that whatever it was, it was a big one. I knew he was not coming to borrow some money. I knew that it was big by that determined look on his face, which I have seen so often through the years. I knew he was not coming to ask for my advice or permission.

This is why I said earlier that when the minister said that Charlie Payne, Daniel's grandfather, always acted on his feelings and had a lot of drive and determination, this was going to affect our lives in a couple of weeks back in Paris. Daniel had a huge love and respect for his grandfather, and he had heard what that minister said … and it had affected him.

So I said, "Hi, what's up?" He said, "Valerie and I are getting married." He had learned from Priscilla how to get to the point and to use few words.

Yep, it was a big one! I said, "Congratulations, that is wonderful. So where is Valerie?" He said, "She is in the lobby." I said, "Well, go get her, so we can call your mother and Sunshine to tell them the good news." I was thrilled as we had already known Valerie for some time, and we thought she was terrific.

Priscilla had predicted back in 1991 that we would have a French daughter-in-law when Daniel moved to France after college. I said, "Why do you predict that?" Priscilla said, "Lee, you fall in love where you live and your son is 22 and living in Paris."

It was 2:00pm in the United States, so I promptly picked up the phone and called Priscilla to tell her that her son was getting married. She said, "I knew he was. I could feel it during the memorial service for my dad." I was thinking, "How do women do that?" I hadn't picked up any vibes at all, and I had never thought back in 1991 that he would marry a French woman. "How do women do this?" I want to learn this.

Priscilla has told me a couple of times that my awareness factor of what is going on around me is low. I think she may be on to something. I joke with her from time to time by telling her that it is not my fault. We men are just a billion or so years behind women, and one day we will catch up. Evolution has been a little slower for us, I tell her. The main point that I was trying to get her to accept was that it is that it is not our fault! I don't think I was successful.

Now once again you are asking yourself, "Why is Lee telling us all of this? What does this have to do with career development?" I am going to tell you later how all of this comes nicely together and all makes sense under the subject of Career

Magic. You will have to wait to learn the secret of how *life puts you through experiences and situations that don't make sense at the time, but in the end, things often turn out perfect. It is how the game ends that is important; it does not matter if you are behind during the game.*

It is now March 1993. I have been working for 28 years. We have moved 10 times since we were married 24 years ago. I am in my 21st job and about to become a father-in-law.

I estimate that these last 3 years have contributed at least $3 million to my experience account, and I now have $10 million in experience. By the way I would put father-in-law down as a significant promotion in my life right, after husband and father.

Next, I'll tell you about another unexpected great ride on the Big Career Roller Coaster that was about to happen.

8

THE MAGICAL DISNEY WORLD YEARS

1993–2006

Daniel had just come to tell me that he and Valerie were getting married. It was March 1993. When we went to France in 1990, I expected to be there at least 5 years. We had been there 3 years; I have not been fired, even if we are losing so much money, so I figured that I was safe, for a while anyway. Actually, I never even thought about losing my job. I am not sure why that did not cross my mind, but it never did. It probably should have, but by now I was a business-war veteran! I would have won the Purple Heart if there were one awarded in business, as I had been wounded many times in my career and survived. Some of my wounds were physical, but most were mental.

The wedding date for Valerie and Daniel had been set for April 24, 1993. In France when you get married you have the ceremony in the Town Hall of the village you live in, and the mayor marries you. Daniel and Valerie would get married in the village of Tigeaux, which is the small village they lived in at the time, a short distance from Euro Disney. He is probably the only American ever married in that village.

Valerie's father, Victor, told Daniel that the first American he had met gave him a chocolate bar at the end of World War II, and the second one was taking his daughter away. By the way, he loved Daniel, the father of his three grandchildren, who live in America. He is luckier than I am in that he has three other grandchildren in France as well. I thought Victor's comment was a pretty neat thing to be able to say.

I remember seeing those movies of American soldiers giving out chocolate bars to the kids as they liberated France.

It was soon arranged for all of us to get together, so the two families could meet each other with the wedding only a few weeks away. Valerie's parents drove up to Paris from their home in a small village near Lyon. We all gathered one Wednesday night and had a wonderful evening together. One thing I love about France is that they open a bottle of champagne for every celebration, no matter how big or small the celebration is.

Priscilla translated for four hours. Victor and I just drank our champagne and smiled since he did not speak English and I did not speak French. Priscilla and Valerie's mother, Anna, kept up the conversation all evening as Victor and I just nodded from time to time and enjoyed our champagne. After that evening together and that marriage, we had some new traditions in our family. When anyone in our family went to France, I would send Victor a bottle of California wine and he would send me back a bottle of French wine.

At Thanksgiving we added a cheese course to the menu in honor of our French daughter-in-law, Valerie. If you have ever wondered why some dishes served at your home on holidays are unique to your family, look back to see who married whom and where they were from. Ask your grandparents, as they probably know the history of that dish. Grandparents are wise and know everything.

As you probably know, the French make lots of jokes about Americans and the Americans make lots of jokes about the French. It is funny how when you have a French daughter-in-law and three perfect, adorable grandchildren who are half French you don't find those jokes amusing in the least. The lesson is that we should not be joking about other people, for many reasons—a big one is that one of those other people might become part of your family one day. This is your diversity lesson for the day, and one that I have learned well.

A couple of weeks after learning of the upcoming marriage of Daniel and Valerie, I got a call from my boss Sanjay telling me Al Weiss wanted to talk with me about a job in Orlando at Walt Disney World. I asked when the job would be available and sure enough, it was available right away. I immediately made sure everyone understood that I could not start any new job until after the wedding to be held on April 24. Talking about tradition. All of these years I thought that I would not have to pay for a wedding because I had a son and not a daughter. Well I quickly learned that in France, it is the custom to share the cost of the wedding. It was a tiny anti-perk, but well worth it.

Daniel and Valerie had what I think was the perfect wedding. On Saturday afternoon April 24, 1993, they were married by the assistant mayor in the Town Hall of the village they lived in. The mayor was supposed to marry them, but his wife died the day before the wedding and the assistant mayor had to step in. They were not married in a church because Daniel was not Catholic. If he had been, then they would have had two ceremonies: one religious and one legal.

After the ceremony, we went to their house and had cake and, of course, Champagne! That evening, the wedding party, which was made up of 20 family and friends, went to the Jules Verne restaurant in the Eiffel Tower for a wonderful dinner and then on Sunday, there was the big reception for all of the friends and family of both families and coworkers. Why I say this was perfect is that we were able to spend the evening before with the bride and groom and their families and closest friends, unlike what is possible when you have one of those big receptions right after the ceremony where the parents never get to see their sons or daughters. Remember the movie, *The Father of the Bride?*

Even before the wedding took place, I had boarded a flight to Orlando to interview with new Executive Vice President, Al

Weiss of the Walt Disney World® Resorts. I never made it to Orlando the day I was supposed to since we could not land in Atlanta to change planes because the biggest snowstorm ever hit the East Coast, including Atlanta. Our flight was diverted to Dallas where I spent two days in a dumpy motel before I could get a flight out to Orlando.

Al and I had our interview, and he offered me the job so I headed back to Paris for the wedding and to tie up all of the loose ends with moving. It was agreed that I would start in May after the late-April wedding. I liked Al right away because I mentioned to him that I like to go work out around 5:30pm every day, and I did not want him coming to my office thinking that I wasn't committed to my job. He explained that he really believes in balance and that he, too, often would be off coaching his daughter's baseball team or his son's basketball team—and for sure, he would never miss any of their school events or games. I loved this man the more he talked. Where had he been all of my life? The lesson here is to make sure you are doing everything possible for those around you to ensure they are able to attend those special family events in their lives.

Back in Paris they had already held the management going-away party for me, but had planned another going-away afternoon event in early May on a Saturday. It was at my boss's house with everyone including husbands, wives, and the kids of my coworkers as guests. All events in my opinion are more fun when there are children present.

I received a call from Al to fly back over for a meeting where it would be announced that I would be the new senior vice

217

president for Walt Disney World® Resorts Operations. He wanted me to be there when the announcement was made so that I could immediately meet with the team, and they would know who I was. My intention was to fly over, attend the announcement meeting and get right back to Paris for the Saturday afternoon going-away party.

I flew over with no problems, and we did the announcement. I was all ready to fly back to Paris to get ready to move in a couple of weeks and to attend my going-away party. Well that was a good plan, but my flight had equipment problems and I spent the next day and night in Raleigh, North Carolina. They had the party in Paris without me in attendance. Just another normal day on the *Big Career/Life Roller Coaster*, but I attended the party for ten minutes by telephone.

I started at the Walt Disney World® Resort on May 23, 1993, as senior vice president of operations for the hotels. Priscilla stayed behind and came in June. I was 48 years old. I had been working for 28 years. Daniel was staying in France with his new wife of course. This would be our 11th move in 25 years. We would be living in Orlando, which was a place I never thought I would live. *You just never know where that Big Career/Life Roller Coaster is going to take you.*

Meg Crofton, who until 2015 was President of Disney Parks and Resorts for the U.S. and France, along with Dale Stafford, who recently retired from Disney after many, many years, were going to be vice presidents of resort operations and would be reporting to me. I came to Orlando, met them and off we went putting together a new, organizational structure.

In those days the resorts, parks, and all support operations were run as separate operations with their own executives. That was far different than it is today where Disney World has an organizational structure in place that enables all areas to work as one team in order to move more quickly and run the Walt Disney World® Resort as one place, as one team!

The very first thing we had to deal with was a business downturn, and we were in meetings thinking about numerous ways to save money. We came up with lots of good ideas that are still in place today. We decided not to change the sheets every day since the guests couldn't have cared less, helped with environmental issues too by not using all of that water and putting all of those chemicals down the drain. We eliminated many layers of management during this time like resident managers, executive chefs, and food and beverage managers of resorts. Disney World can thank me for putting in an email system in 1993 when I got there. The Walt Disney World® Resort did not have email at the time, even though we had it in France. You actually may thank me or curse me; once you get used to having it, it is hard to get along without it.

I started teaching time management right away as a forum for people to get to know me. I scheduled several large meetings in the evenings for 200 to 300 managers, so they could see my face and hear my philosophy. I had them fax in any question they wanted me to answer, because that email system was not in place yet. They sent me lots of tough questions, and I answered every one of them. I wanted to get all of the rumors and guessing out of the way. I guess this was the forerunner of what Disney now calls the *New Leader Transition* sessions, which are encouraged by all leaders to have when taking on a new role. The New Leader Transition is really gathering everyone in one room and letting the new leader explain how he or she works, how they like to be communicated with and to clarify their expectations. It speeds up by months with everyone getting on the same page. Al and I did a retreat with all of the executives and did a New Leader Transition with them as well. This is a very effective tool that I wish I had learned about earlier in my career. It just plain speeds up people getting to know you, what you want, how you work, and what is important to you.

In 1995 I created the *Disney Great Leader Strategies,* and somewhere along the way promoted Dieter Hannig to director and then to vice president of food and beverage. Our food and beverage reputation soared after that one decision. I told Al Weiss once that I should get all of the credit for our world-class food and beverage reputation because I put Dieter in the job. He smiled and said, "And I put you in your job!" I am pretty sure that was a compliment.

Senior Vice President of Merchandise, Joan Ryan, had just joined the company before I came to Orlando. Through the years, Joan reported to everyone, and finally to me as we pulled all operations under one structure. She is another leader who created a world-class reputation for Disney in the retail merchandise business. Joan can tell you a lot about the *Big Career Life Roller Coaster,* as can Dieter Hannig, Bud Dare, Erin Wallace, Karl Holz, Alice Norsworthy and Jeff Vahle. Actually,

I think if you spoke to every one of my direct reports, you would find they each had some difficult and exciting rides on that Big Roller Coaster. I know that Don Robinson, Liz Boice, Rich Taylor, Greg Emmer, Michael Colglazier, and the three people in my office, Chris Bostick, Marsha Davis, and Jeanette Manent, have had their own ups and downs on this exciting ride. Today they are all doing a great job and have their roller coasters under control … for the moment anyway.

This is a good lesson on how important it is to get the right people in the right roles. Every one of my direct reports took us from just okay to great over the years. I was blessed with a world-class team. I never worried about our ability to implement anything regardless of how challenging it may have seemed at the moment. 9/11 proved me right on this count. Without this team, we could never have accomplished what we did in such a short period of time … leadership matters!

This team, including me, learned to appreciate one another and share the leadership position, as it made sense. There are few teams, if any, who can do this the way we did and it's why we achieved spectacular results on any issue or project we took on. We had total and complete respect for one another as individuals as well as professionals.

In 1996 we received Michael Eisner's approval to spend $6 million to renovate the then Top of the World restaurant at Disney's Contemporary Resort and make a new restaurant there called the California Grill. This one decision moved us down the path to food and beverage excellence. After that conversion we now had a lab to show what we could do. Many other new and exciting concepts followed which increased our reputation over the years. Bad food and service are against the law now at the Walt Disney World® Resort. Again the best talent made the California Grill exceptional. Without Clifford Pleau, the chef who I hired for the California Grill in Paris at the Disneyland Hotel, and George Miliotes, the restaurant manager, we would have just been a good restaurant. They made it great! The difference between good and great is so big that it can't be understood until it's experienced.

A few years later through Joan Ryan's determination, we built a very large World of Disney Store at Downtown Disney. Everyone thought it should be a smaller store except Joan … and she was right. This is one of the greatest stores in the world. Without her persistence, we would have built a store much smaller and never have realized what we have today.

Don Robinson came back from France after being the general manager of the Newport Bay Hotel at Euro Disney where we first worked together. He started as the opening general manager of Disney's All-Star Resort upon his return to Orlando. He had already been Director of Rooms for the Resorts Division. Little did he know or even imagine back then that he would be the top executive who would open Hong Kong Disneyland one day. He also didn't realize that he would soon be married to Suzy Elrod. Ask Don about the excitement and thrill of the *Big Career/Life Roller Coaster*. He has had his ups and downs like all of us.

You see, *everyone has to do it his or her own way.* Don had never worked for anyone else but Disney for 30+ years, but he kept up with what was going on in the world and never quit learning. He went on to open the Hong Kong project and then left Disney and had a very successful 7 years as President of Baha Mar Resort in the Bahamas and then as COO before retiring from All Aboard Florida, the new high speed train which will run 32 times a day between Miami and Orlando. The business skills Don learned at Disney served him well.

I held the position of senior vice president of operations for the Walt Disney World® Resorts from 1993 to 1995.

In 1995, Al Weiss was promoted to executive vice president for all of the Walt Disney World® Resort which included all of the theme parks, and resorts as well as Downtown Disney and the ESPN Sports Complex. Not long after that he was promoted to President. I was promoted to senior vice president of operations for the Walt Disney World® Resort. I reported to Bruce Laval, Executive Vice President of Operations for Walt Disney World® Operations.

We began the process of putting the entire Walt Disney World® Resort organization under one structure, reporting up to Al Weiss. This would be the first time that all of the businesses were under the responsibility of one person in such an organized way. This would begin the journey to stimulate teamwork and movement of leaders among all of the businesses at the Walt Disney World® Resort. This turned out to be the best decision we ever made. It was not done without some pain and some resistance, but it was accomplished and was the right thing to do. *Remember that resistance is not a good reason to stop something that you believe in. Anytime you're about to do some-*

thing hard, expect resistance. I had a lot to learn since I knew nothing about the parks. Early on, I knew there were many Disney veterans who wondered why I was even given the job.

Slowly, but surely, we got the place more and more organized to be efficient and effective. This was the era in which strict cost management and productivity targets were developed. While many of you may not like the cost management and productivity-target process, it is one of the most important processes a business can have in place as long as it is managed in a balanced and flexible way. Every business has to improve its productivity every year. There is always a better way or a new technology to help with this. *As long as you balance productivity with employee excellence and guest satisfaction, you will achieve the right business results over the long term.*

In May 1997, I was promoted to executive vice president of Walt Disney World® Operations. Now all support groups and operating groups fell under one organizational structure, and we started to make big progress.

- During these years, we learned how important a clear organizational structure was, as well as the importance of hiring right-fit talent.

- During these years, we learned the value of using structured interviews before hiring someone, and we worked with the Gallup organization to refine this work. This was an exciting and important thing for me to learn. I wish I had known about structured interviews earlier in my career. We became much more careful about the selection of leaders.

- We took on very controversial issues—such as elim-inating leads (supervisors)—differently than we had ever done before.

- We did so much over a few years to improve the Walt Disney World® Resort that I sometimes find it hard to believe that we accomplished so much so fast. When you have a great team you can go faster.

- We implemented the Cast Excellence Survey during this time to measure cast satisfaction with leadership, culture and resources they needed to do their jobs well.

- We also improved our guest satisfaction research dramatically.

- We taught everyone the importance of not only be-ing a good leader, but that we all need to be great. We knew that our fellow cast members deserved great leadership, so they could deliver world-class service to our guests. The importance of great leadership is one thing I know for sure to be the silver bullet for attain-ing excellent results in any endeavor. I wish that I had understood this earlier in my career.

I had been in my current role for almost 10 years as of July 2006 and had been reporting to Al Weiss for 13 years. I tell people it was almost like being married. He knows me well, and I know him well. He leads me as an individual, he makes me feel special, he respects me … and he has made me much more knowledgeable. I hope you have a leader like that. It is a lot more fun and satisfying.

I am part of a Steering Committee Team that has been together for a long time, and we work well together. We had a real test of teamwork after 9/11 and again after the hurricanes hit Orlando in 2004. We had been through challenging times together before, but nothing like 9/11!

Al showed what he was made of during this crisis, as did every member of the Steering Committee. Al took charge and gave us direction while staying cool, calm, and collected. This is exactly what you want in a crisis. This is no time to try to gain consensus. During a crisis, you need one leader and you need one who acts fast.

I read recently that during World War II Winston Churchill set up a separate organization outside the normal bureaucracy to do one thing, and that was to tell him the truth. Smart Man! (This is what Chapter 8, Strategy #6 explains in detail in my first book, *Creating Magic*. The title of this chapter is, "Learn The Truth."

We continued to tweak the organizational structure frequently to make sure we were putting right-fit talent in place by following all of the *Disney Great Leader Strategies*. I learned at the Walt Disney World® Resort to pay better attention to the data instead of everyone's personal opinion. Many of the changes we have made over the years were fought and resisted internally and externally because people just hate change. We kept a keen eye on our guest satisfaction scores versus all of the noise from people who may have an unknown agenda or just don't want a change to happen. While personal opinion is interesting, it is neither quantitative nor reliable by itself.

We prepared for and went through the infamous Y2K year, and we all held our breath on December 31, 1999, wondering if the whole world, which had become dependent on computers for everything would shut down. *Nothing at all happened anywhere!* Nothing even happened in countries that did not prepare. That day I watched on television every time zone in the world celebrated the arrival of the year 2000. I wrote a record of it for my grandchildren as it happened. It was a good quiet day without incident.

We have had sad times too as we lost some of our fellow cast members. I remember with sadness our Steering Committee having lunch with Frank Wells, President of The Walt Disney Company, on Good Friday and seeing on television two days later on Easter Sunday that he had been killed in a helicopter accident. He was a great man.

Over the years we made great strides in diversity and inclusiveness. We had a long way to go, but we stayed focused on this vital issue of respecting, appreciating, and valuing everyone. This is one of the most important things you can do for your fellow employees, guests/customers, and your business. My big learning experience here was that I personally had to step up to this responsibility in order to make it happen. By using my position, authority, and communication skills to convince others to get engaged and be proactive, we could create the right culture and environment for everyone. I had to take a public position on diversity as did many other leaders at the Walt Disney World® Resort. I hope you have. You cannot stand in the shadows on this subject if you are in a leadership position.

I learned more in those 16 years at Disney than I did during the first 25 years of my career, and I think I still have many things to learn. I had now been working for 41 years. I had been with Disney for 16 years on July 8, 2006. I have three grandchildren who lived a mile away from me. I had been married 35 years and we had relocated 11 times. Priscilla got her first new car ever when we moved to Orlando in June 1993. We agreed we would buy it if she would drive it for 10 years. She drove it for 13 years. (I thought I would show you how big of a heart I have by telling you that I finally bought her a new car!) We love Orlando. We love Disney … and in fact, Priscilla told me a few years ago, "Lee, behave and don't get fired because I like it here."

I calculate that these last 16 years at the Walt Disney World® Resort has added at least another $5 million to my experience account, which puts the total value of my experience at $15 million. *The value of experience is safe. It is yours forever. It cannot go down in value like the stock market or a house, so it's a worthwhile venture to invest a lot in this area.*

In Chapter 9 I'll sum up of this up by explaining why everything that has happened to me in my *Big Career/Life Roller Coaster* ride has turned out well … SO FAR!

9

LIFE AFTER DISNEY
2006–PRESENT

WOW! **THAT WAS A FAST RIDE** on the *Big Career Life Roller Coaster.* This ride started eight chapters ago when I was just 20 years old, single, broke, and had just been discharged from the United States Army. I had dropped out of college and secured my first position in the hospitality field as a banquet waiter at the about-to-open, new Washington Hilton Hotel in Washington, D.C.

And now, here it was May 2006 and I am 62 years old. I had been married for 38 years to Priscilla; we have a 37-year-old son, Daniel, a French daughter-in law, Valerie and three perfect and adorable grandchildren by the names of Jullian Charles, Margot Sunshine, and Tristan Lee. I particularly like

Tristan's middle name. When your children give their children your name, you know you're getting old.

I am in my 24th professional position. Priscilla and I have moved 11 times. I have worked for three large and famous companies over these last 41 years: Hilton Hotels for 8 years, Marriott International for 17 years, and The Walt Disney Company for 16 years. I am now the senior operations executive at Walt Disney World and responsible for all operations. I have a dream job. I have the job everyone would love to have. I have the job I never ever imagined back in 1965 that I could attain. When I started my career with Hilton, Disney World was not even open yet.

Our eleven moves have included some very interesting and wonderful cities, and we enjoyed every place we lived except one and we were only there 90 days before I was fired. Our moves in order were: Washington, D.C., Chicago, New York City, Tarrytown, New York, Los Angeles, Lancaster, Pennsylvania, Philadelphia, Chicago, Washington, D.C., Springfield, Massachusetts, Paris, France, and finally Orlando.

What I did next, at the pinnacle of my career surprised a lot of people. I left Disney and decided not to pursue positions in other large organizations. I announced my retirement from Disney to be effective July 28, 2006. I decided there must be more to life than working for big corporations. I am suffering again from that ailment called boredom. I have been doing the same job for almost 10 years.

I decided I wanted to have my own company, no boss, no politics, no cost management targets, no Power Point presentations, no late night budget meetings, no nothing, except what I wanted to do every morning when I climbed out of bed. I decided I wanted to become a writer, public speaker and teacher. I had been writing for many years and believed that I had a lot of knowledge and experience to share with others, which could add great value to their professional and personal lives. Someone once told me there are three ways to leave a legacy: have a baby, write a book or plant a tree. I still need to plant a tree to leave three legacies. You don't leave a legacy by attaining some high level position with a for- profit company unless you were a great teacher and helped lots of people be better and more successful than they ever imagined they could be. The other way was that you did something that changed the world, like Steve Jobs or Walt Disney—*your legacy will not be what job you held, but what you did for others.*

Al Weiss organized a wonderful retirement party for me. A lot of my team members and other people got up and said a lot of nice things about me and about my leadership, but the highlight for my retirement was that a window on Main Street USA in the Magic Kingdom was dedicated to me. It is the window right above Uptown Jewelers. I also was given a custom made, four-foot-high Mickey that had been designed and manufactured in the Central Shops at Disney. It was named Hurricane Mickey because Mickey is wearing a yellow rain slicker with a flashlight in one hand and a cell phone in the other hand. Jeff Vahle, the head of maintenance, and his team picked this concept for Mickey to remind me of the many days and nights we all spent in the Disney World Command

Center managing Disney World through the three hurricanes that struck Orlando in 2004.

Before I announced my retirement I had discussions with the Disney Institute executives and with Al Weiss to get an agreement to become an executive speaker for the Disney Institute and to work with the Disney Institute to write a book about Disney leadership principals. Al and the Disney Institute agreed this would be a good partnership. The Disney Institute created the Executive Speaker Series of which Marty Sklar, the former head of Disney Imagineering and a 50-year cast member, along with myself, were members. We were available to speak on behalf of the Disney Institute around the world.

On July 29, 2006, the day after my retirement I started writing my first book, *Creating Magic: 10 Common Sense Leadership Strategies from A Life at Disney.* It took me a little over 2 years to finish the book and to get it published on October 8, 2008. It currently has been published in 14 languages around the world. I hired a New York literary agent, Lynn Franklin, to represent me with publishers in the U.S. and internationally. We eventually selected Random House as the U.S. publisher. I hired a professional writer from California, Phil Goldberg to write a professional book proposal to submit to publishers and then to take my manuscript and make it a great read. I hired former Disney Cast Member John Van Horn to develop a website for me: www.LeeCockerell.com. Jody Maberry manages my *Lessons in Leadership* blog and podcast, *Creating Disney Magic* which is also on iTunes, Stitcher Radio and iHeart Radio in addition to my website. I hired a couple out of Toronto, Deidra Jones and her husband Robert Maran, to develop my leadership app, *Creating Magic: Leadership and Coaching on the Go* which is available for iPhones and now under development for Android. I hired a computer expert, Greg Clayton, to take care of my computer problems and to teach me how to be more proficient in how to use my computer. I worked with the University of Central Florida (UCF) to design and print a workbook for my seminars. This workbook is titled, *Lessons in Leadership, Management and Customer Service.* I use this workbook to teach day-long or two-day workshops around the world. I am different than every other speaker on the circuit; I don't use PowerPoint and my audiences love it. *Find ways to stand out and to be different than everyone else.*

Once again, a big and perhaps most important lesson in Career Magic, is to surround yourself with experts who are great at what they do and who have the ability to make you great too. I also hired an expert personal trainer, Andrew Noble, to keep me fit. I have been working with him since 2010 twice a week and today I am stronger than when I was 20 years old and after the age of 50, strength is more important than aerobics if you don't want to fall and break a hip and be in a wheelchair or use a walker for the last years of your life, if you survive the fall.

In 2012, Random House called me and told me they would like me to write another book since *Creating Magic* was doing so well. At first I was not interested in doing that. Writing a book is a lot of work and I was retired, sort of. We continued to talk and I eventually agreed to write my second book on customer service, *The Customer Rules: The 39 Essential Rules for Delivering Sensational Service.* It only took Phil Goldberg and me nine months to finish. We published *The Customer Rules* on March 15, 2013. It has been published in 10 languages so far. Many public schools, colleges and universities are using these books in the classroom. We developed a teacher's guide for *Creating Magic and for Time Management Magic* for college professors and will have a teacher's guide soon for *The Customer Rules.*

My current work includes public speaking, giving keynote speeches, and day-long seminars to organizations around the world on leadership, management and customer service as well as working with the Disney Institute for 10 years.

One of the best things that I became involved in since retiring is volunteering my time to work with all branches of our military. I first spoke to 20 Army Generals 16 years ago at a leadership conference being held by the chief of staff of the Army at Disney's Yacht Club Resort. Over the years I have continued to work with them. I even had the privilege of going to Iraq during the war in 2011 to present 13 workshops on leadership, management and customer service to troops all over Iraq from North to South and to State Department Employees in the Embassy in Baghdad. Before that a few years back I even had the opportunity to do a tandem parachute jump with the Golden Knight Army Parachute Team.

I am now working with a group to launch our new online learning site for entrepreneurs: *www.Thrive15.com.* The site has hundreds of 15-minute entertaining videos on how to do everything from hiring to firing; from formulating interviews to how to be a better leader, a better manager and have world class customer service in your organization. For every paid subscription we give a free subscription to a veteran. Check it out and use the promotion code: MAGIC for a free 30-day trial.

Another great learning website that I am a part of is *www.TheSportsMindInstitute.com*. Here you can learn from me and a long list of well-known and successful sports figures. There are bulk discounts available for both of these sites.

So as you can see, there is life after dropping out of college, life after the U.S. Army, life after Hilton, life after being fired, life after being passed over for that big promotion at Marriott, and life after Disney.

Conclusions and What I Have Learned Along The Way

We have made many friends as we've moved around the world, and many are still good friends today. We learned a lot about the world, and I think this travel opportunity was one of the best diversity educations I could ever have received. The more places you live and the more cultures and people you experience, the more tolerant you become. I have learned the value of education, experience, and travel as important advantages to self-development.

One thing for sure is that each place has its own style of pizza. It may not always be called pizza, but it is always some kind of dough with a choice of many toppings or dips whether you are in Chicago, India, Iraq, Portugal, Kuwait or France. I think that breads define each place you live somehow. The Best baguettes and croissants are definitely in France though.

The journey so far in my career has included many things:

- There have been moments of great joy and satisfaction as well as moments of uncertainty and disappointment.
- There have been times when I was on top of the world and times when I was at the bottom of the barrel.
- There have been times when I wasn't sure how we might pay for this or that and times when I wondered if I had just made the biggest mistake of my life.
- There have been times I have made lots of bad decisions in jobs, investments, relationships, and the way I treated people.

I was one of those people who never had a career plan. I had no 5-year goals or ever even contemplated reaching the positions I have attained over the years. I am as surprised as much as my high-school teachers are that I am where I am today. I am sure they would tell you that this couldn't be the same Lee Cockerell who went to Ardmore High School and made mostly C's and D's?

My basic philosophy for success was to perform each position I had better than anyone else, and it seemed as I did this that every now and then I would receive a promotion. My mother taught me this hard work ethic … so thanks, Mom.

I was usually the most surprised when these opportunities were offered to me. I always took the next position and just did the best work I could. I never made any noise about wanting the next thing or the next promotion because I was usually surprised that I had the job that I had. Most of my career, I had just plugged along and the opportunity would show up just about the time that I was prepared to take it on.

One reason I have had so much professional success is that I married a saint—or should I say, she agreed to marry me? Without Priscilla's understanding of not only all of the moves but also the long hours and stressful moments from time to time, I am sure I would not be where I am today.

One day I said to Priscilla, "Don't you feel bad about not having a career and working all of these years?" She said, "I do not and in fact, if I had not stayed home and taken care of everything in this family, you would not be where you are today. You did not have to worry about anything at home and that left you the time and energy to focus on your career."

She has always been very clear and to the point. I never had thought about it that way, but I decided it was true after I gave it some thought for a while. With a career in the hospitality business and especially all of those years in food and beverage, my hours were long and the number of days I had to work each week was unpredictable. Priscilla did a world-class job of raising our son, Daniel.

One time I was talking to someone about the long hours that I worked, and this person said to me, "Lee, it is not your profession only that requires long hours. People who are successful in any endeavor usually work long hours whether they are the best insurance agent in town, the best car salesman, the best lawyer, the best minister, an Admiral in the Navy, the best secretary, the best student, the best teacher, the best restaurant manager, the best mom or dad, the best grandparent, the best general manager, and so on. I am sorry to have to tell you, that to achieve a high level of success in any endeavor you usually have to work hard at it." The best athletes practice after practice. They work harder than anyone else.

I hear over and over again how this generation or that generation doesn't want to work too much and that they want more time off and things are not the way they used to be. I don't believe that completely. I do believe, however, that most individuals want a more balanced life between their professional and personal life.

I want that too, and I believe that you can have both, but to achieve both, you really have to work hard at being organized and not think about balance only as the number of hours you spend on the job or on personal things, but about what you do with the hours you have each day. If you are struggling with managing your life, then you should probably buy my book, *Time Management Magic*. This book is more than just about time management. It should be called Time/Life Management, as it really teaches how to manage your life rather than just your time. Your goal is to keep your whole life under control.

My two favorite Einstein quotes are:
- "The value of a man should be seen in what he gives and not in what he is able to receive."
- "Two things are infinite: the universe and human stupidity; and I'm not sure about the universe."

My *Lessons in Leadership Blog* and *Creating Magic Podcast,* if I do say so myself, gives good weekly advice and points on how to think about creating Career Magic and the successful management of your personal life away from the job. I suggest you take time to read the blog and listen to the podcasts at www.LeeCockerell.com.

It should take you no more than 5 minutes to read my blogs and 15 minutes a week to listen to my podcast which seems to me to be a small amount of time to put into learning more about the profession you have chosen. If you are a professional leader, I believe that you have the responsibility to continuously develop yourself in the areas of:

- Technical competence
- Management skills
- Technological competence
- Relational competence
- Leadership competence

These are the areas that you should be thinking about every day. You have got to convince yourself what you believe about leadership and how you are going to practice it. Studying leadership is one way to fully develop your own beliefs, which will translate into the way you practice leadership.

This is a basic concept that you—if you want to be a successful leader—must come to grips with.

- What are you doing to improve in these five areas every day, month, and year?

- What are you reading about in the areas of leadership and management?
- What courses are you taking to improve yourself?
- What weaknesses do you have that could be improved through training, coaching, and counseling?
- Are you working on these weaknesses? Have you reviewed my books, *Creating Magic, The Customer Rules,* and *Time Management Magic* lately to do a self-analysis of what you do well and what things you need to improve in?

The main responsibility that all people in leadership positions have is to create a positive culture and environment for their fellow employees so they are able to perform to the level of their capability.

- Where they are made to feel special
- Where they feel they are treated as individuals
- Where they feel they are respected
- Where you, the leader, help make them more knowledgeable, develop them, and help them understand their role technically, physically, and emotionally.

We call this environment that leaders can create *"employee excellence."* This simply means that you, the leader, have created a culture and environment where each employee is involved in his or her work. It's an environment that is where each employee can perform his or her role at the highest level possible for them as individuals. Leaders who excel at creating this culture and environment are able to achieve the greatest results in employee excellence, guest/customer satisfaction, and business.

This is common sense, but so many leaders don't focus on it for many reasons. Some leaders get so focused on the technical side of their role that they just don't pay attention to people. This eventually catches up with them whether they know it or not. Often they just don't get as far along in their careers as they would like to and often don't really know why. Remember the saying, "Don't be the fool who forgets that it gets done through people." It is just amazing to me how anyone who is a leader cannot figure out this simple concept. *The problem is that when leaders worry more about themselves and their own success than they do about their people, the right culture and environment are not in place.* The leader and his or her fellow employees all suffer, as do your guests/customers and your business results.

Being disorganized and not able to get things done is the other big problem so many leaders suffer from. Technological competence is important, but its necessity is low compared to the importance of leadership and management competence … unless, I guess, if you are an IT professional, and then you need the expertise to get in the door.

Technical competence, on the other hand, is hardly ever a big problem, as most people know how to do what they are supposed to do; however if they are disorganized and have poor leadership competency, they have trouble getting it done, and that's the problem.

It really does not matter how well-educated you are, where you went to school, or how technically competent you are; if you can't get anything done—or if you achieve far less than your potential because you do not leverage your fellow employees to find their true potential—then you have a long way to go as a leader. If you can't inspire your fellow employees and build trust with them, you will not be able to get the best possible results.

I have learned some of these things the hard way through my career, and others came naturally. I do know if I had had the level of training in all of these areas right off the bat in my career that Marriott and Disney provided I would have been a much better and effective leader earlier.

10

THE SCARIEST
RIDE OF MY LIFE
AND FINAL THOUGHTS

2008–2016

HERE **I** AM, *having the perfect life.* I am retired now for 2 years. I have finished writing my first book. My consulting, teaching and speaking business is going well. I am healthy and confident about the future—until August 6, 2008, when my whole world started to fall apart. Priscilla had not been feeling well for a week or so. On Sunday she told me her stomach was really hurting and I needed to take here to the emergency room.

Within 10 minutes we were at the Dr. Phillips Hospital Emergency Room. By the time we arrived Priscilla could not even sit in a chair because of the pain. She ended up lying on the floor so she could spread out and eliminate some of the discomfort. The staff did a quick CT scan and found that she had two abscesses on her colon. She had had issues with diverticulitis for years but nothing as serious as this. The doctor admitted her to the hospital.

Over the next two weeks they pumped her full of powerful antibiotics and finally brought the infections under control so she could be discharged and sent home where nurses came for another 30 days to administer more antibiotics. After all of this life slowly returned to normal … but not for long.

During the next check-up, the doctor told Priscilla that she needed to have a resection of her sigmoid colon to avoid future recurrences. We scheduled that surgery for August 6, 2008. At 11:00am that same morning I finished recording the audio version of my first book, *Creating Magic,* and went right to the hospital to see Priscilla before she went into surgery. I gave her a kiss and off she went.

This was the beginning of a 2-year nightmare. The surgery lasted for 3½ hours. Priscilla stayed in the hospital for 5 days and I took her home on August 11. By the morning of the 13th she was in a lot of pain and to this day she does not remember much about what happened that day.

I called her doctor's office and was told to take her back to the hospital and they would call to have her admitted. Here is a time management story for you. The doctor told me I could take her right now or wait until later that afternoon. I immediately took her to the hospital and got her registered.

A Visit To No Man's Land
If I had waited until later that afternoon she would not be here today. We were registered in the hospital but there were no rooms available, as no patients had been discharged yet. We were put in a long hallway on a gurney outside the Emergency Room where no one treated Priscilla. We were in a Catch-22, in "no man's land." Doctors and nurses were everywhere but no one would treat her because you either have to be in the emergency room or in a hospital room to be treated.

Leaders Step Up When You Least Expect It
I learned that day and for the next 2 years a good lesson about leadership—leaders step up when you least expect it and do the right things no matter how hard it is.

The first leader in this 2-year horror story showed up when we needed him most. A doctor exiting the emergency room to go on break came toward us. I stopped him and told him what was going on and how Priscilla was being readmitted to the hospital after her resection surgery earlier in the week, but no rooms were available. I explained to him that no one was treating her and that she was in severe pain and needed pain medication and she needed to be hydrated. He looked at me with concern but said, "I am not supposed to do that." I said why? He said you are not in the emergency room. What he was trying to say, but did not, was that this would cause a big legal issue. I told him I understood but that she really needs some attention right now. I will never forget how he said, "Okay, I will do it." That is what leaders do. They step up and do the right thing versus worry about legal issues or anything else, including their personal safety. As they say, bravery is about being scared and doing it any way. I suspect this doctor saved Priscilla's life. He examined Priscilla, got her some pain meds and got an IV in her.

Priscilla was admitted a couple of hours later. The doctor examined her and told me that since Priscilla was now sleeping and all of her vital signs were perfect that I should just go on home and they would do CT scan since it could not be that serious. I went home.

When I came back to the hospital at 7:00am the next morning and went to Priscilla's room, she wasn't there. It took about 15 minutes for a nurse to find out where she was and to inform me that she was in the Intensive Care Unit. That was the longest 15 minutes of my life.

It turns out that she had emergency surgery after the CT scan showed that her first surgery had failed. She woke up seven days later on a ventilator with a colostomy and a wound VAC that she would have to wear for the next 5 months because of the infection from the failed bowel resection surgery 8 days earlier.

I won't tell you all of the gory details of what we went through for the next 18 months but I will tell you that we ran into real leaders over and over and over again from incredible nurses and doctors that went way beyond the call of duty to techs, housekeepers and cafeteria staff that stepped up time and time again to do more than they were required to do.

Priscilla spent a total of 64 days in the hospital and the bill was over $700,000 dollars before adjustments with the insurance company. I have to tell you that one of the greatest blessings were that we still had Cigna Health Insurance through Disney. Cigna assigned a person to us, which took a lot of weight off of my shoulders. I would give them a score of 10. It could not have been handled any better.

Over the next 18 months I had to take care of Priscilla's every need. She was weak and could not do anything for herself plus "we" had a colostomy and wound VAC to worry about 24/7.

I say "we" because I was intimately involved in these two devices. In addition to this, I also had to get five Ensure protein drinks down her a day (60g of protein) in order to heal, as she had no appetite to eat normal food. She hated them, but I made her drink them. I also had to get her out of bed three times a day at 7:00am, 12 noon and 5:00pm to walk 20 laps through the house with her walker so she would become stronger. She didn't want to do this either, but I insisted and we had a few words from time to time.

We all want to crawl back in bed when we don't feel well. I put a new system in place to ensure she did all 20 laps. I put a table in the hall and called it the tollbooth. I gave Priscilla 20 playing cards and informed her the toll was one card each time she passed by and that I would be sitting at the toll booth working on my computer and collecting the tolls and when I got 20 she could go back to bed. I won't tell you what she said to me …

Priscilla slowly got better and one day she was all back to normal and feeling well, but we still had one really big problem. She feels great, she looks great, her energy is good but she still has a colostomy bag hanging on her left side. Now what do we do? It is a big surgery to take a colostomy down and it is not always successful. We were scared to death until we met another great leader who was considered by many to be one of the best colon rectal surgeons anywhere. We made an appointment to see Paul Williamson. He took three weeks to study Priscilla's medical file, which by this time was five inches thick. We went in to meet with him. He walked into the room and looked at Priscilla and said, "Priscilla, you are going to be fine. You are the kind of patient I love to fix." He then said, "I consider every one of my patients a gift from God and no one will touch you in the operating room but me. I will open you, do the surgery and close you. And I go to the chapel before surgery to get extra help." He went on to tell us that Priscilla needed another three months of healing time before he could do the surgery. That day arrived. Dr. Williamson told us it would be about 4½ hours for surgery. It ended up taking 9½ hours. Every hour a nurse would come out and keep me updated on how it was going and mainly to reassure me that all was well.

When the surgery was finished, Dr. Williamson came out

and told me that Priscilla was fine. I said to him, "Paul, why did it take so long." His answer is what every great leader says when they have done something difficult. He said, "I did what I said I would do, I fixed her and she is going to be fine.

The last and final thing I have to tell you about this saga is that I ended up with anxiety and depression and had to be treated for a year-and-a-half with the drug Cymbalta to get back on track. I was lucky to find a great doctor/leader as well. His name is Roderick Hundley. I went to see him and by then I was in pretty bad shape and hooked on Ativan, a narcotic for lowering anxiety as well as sleeping pills. After interviewing me, Dr. Hundley said the sweetest words I had heard in a long time. He said, "Lee, I predict you are going to be fine. You are suffering from situational depression from the long period of stress you were under with your wife's illness." Those were the same words Dr. Williamson said to Priscilla. Not only did Dr. Hundley give me encouragement he also gave me his cell number and home number and told me I could contact him anytime 24/7 if I was having any issues. Who in the world does that? Leaders do that! He also told me that he was glad I came in as many men don't come in for help. He said women do but men don't and that 80% of depression can be cured today. Lesson here guys—*when you need help, go get it.*

As I arrived at Chapter 10 of this book I was contemplating how to go about ending it and I think I'll finish up by telling you all the things I can remember that I have learned over the years. Hopefully this will give you food for thought as you ride your career roller coaster.

I have learned that in order to have a shot at achieving your goals, you have to take care of your health. The things I have learned in this area are to make exercise part of my daily routine and to schedule it like any other important appointment. If you are serious, this will be in your calendar. I've also learned to schedule my annual physical, because no matter how much you exercise, it's important to take preventative precautions against disease and early detection is critical. Annual eye exams and annual dentist checkups need to be scheduled as well. I almost forgot that we live in Florida, so go see that dermatologist every year too. It's hard to believe that a tiny mole can kill you, but it can.

I know that you are supposed to get your teeth cleaned twice a year, and I do, but I floss every single day, ever since I read that sign in the dentist's office years ago that said, "Only floss the teeth you want to keep." This flossing saves time, money, and extra visits to the dentist, which is just fine with me. Flossing takes about 60 seconds anyway.

Also, gentlemen, make sure you get all of those tests that men hate to get. They are not as bad as the rumors you hear about them, and they are a lot better than the alternative. The survival statistics are not good on the number of men who do not get an annual checkup.

Another thing I have learned is to listen to your doctor and to do what he or she says, like take the right vitamins, stop smoking, lose 25 pounds, and other things that are recommended if you trust him or her. If you don't trust your doctor, then find another doctor. At one point I had been seeing the same doctor for 22 years for my annual physical. I couldn't mislead him because he had my file, and he knew how much I weighed 22 years ago. I now weigh the same as I did in high school. It is hard, but when you do the hard things, life gets easier.

Maintaining the correct weight, I think, is even more important than exercise. If you do both, then that is even better. Keep a pair of pants from when you were 20, and see if you can get into them when you are 30, 40, and 50. For instance, my cholesterol used to be 230. With exercise, it went down to 173. Today, with changes in my diet, it is 136. The proof is in the pudding. The five big tests for men to have at the appropriate ages are cholesterol (avoid bypass and heart attacks), colon (avoid cancer), prostate (avoid cancer), blood pressure (avoid strokes and heart attacks), and glucose (avoid diabetes). Do you know these numbers?

When you get your exam, they will let you know how the other big organs look—like your heart, liver, and kidneys. I'm writing this just to let you know that a large percentage of men don't get an annual physical and often find out too late. Life is short enough already. Don't make it even shorter.

Ladies, I am sorry that I am not as qualified to give you advice; women do a better job usually of looking after their health and having all of the right tests. This is why when you visit nursing homes there are 180 women and 7 men. Harass those men in your life.

One thing that leaders need is high energy, and the bottom line of how to have more is to eat right, get daily exercise, and get enough sleep. In warmer areas especially, make sure you are drinking enough water. When you feel tired, it is often because you are dehydrated, did not get enough sleep, did not exercise, or just ate a big plate of spaghetti, a loaf of Italian garlic bread, and two pieces of cheesecake. I told you that I would tell you everything that I learned. Maybe it will help you.

I learned a really important thing a few years ago when I was 58. For years Priscilla had told me how important it is to stretch and remain flexible. I finally listened to her and now stretch for 10 minutes every day. It was hard at first and no fun. The results are amazing. So, aerobic exercise five days a week, strength training two days a week, and stretching every day—and bingo, you feel a lot better. That is the main reason I can work until I am 85 or longer, if I elect to do so, unless someone or something does me in before then. My current work is my golf game. I enjoy it. Especially when the audience claps. Remember, you have to be alive to make a difference.

What else is important in Career Magic? I think one big thing for me is to help people. Using your leadership position and authority to help people and to be available for people when they need you is a big deal. Leaders have an awesome power over people's lives. A leader can either use his or her position and authority to do good things, to do bad things, or to do nothing. Quit being the big, bad boss and become a teacher.

Rosemary Travis at Gallup, while giving me feedback on my Gallup Leadership profile years ago, said, "Lee, make sure you always use your talent to do good." Pretty good reminder,

I thought.

There are many forks in the road as we travel through life. The leaders, parents and/or professional leaders have the ability to help direct others down the right path so they have a better life than they might have had without direction and assistance.

- Sometimes people just need you to listen.
- Sometimes people just need a little bitty bit of help opening a door for them.
- Sometimes people need a lot of help that will take a lot of your time.

How well leaders do this separates the great leaders and great parents from the mediocre ones.

If you want to leave a legacy in your life, then make a priority of being available for people when they need you. *Help people every chance you get.* You may not always be successful, but the least you can do as a leader is to try.

I have had eight people in my life thus far who have been there for me when I needed them. Some are family, and some are professional associates. I have made it a point to repay them by being there for other people when they need me.

What else have I learned so far? One thing I have learned is to forget about the chain of command. Most of you are not in the military. I try to make it clear with everyone I work with that I will talk to whomever I want to talk to and that I expect for people to talk to me directly and to keep me informed directly without ever worrying about the chain of command. The chain of command slows things down significantly and delivers less reliable facts and information. The translation and emotion of an issue are never translated or passed on properly. I am not saying to disregard your leader first and not give him or her a chance when you have a problem, but I am saying that working through the chain of command does not always work.

Leaders who worry about the chain of command structure are usually insecure people, who are trying to be in control for some reason. I think it is fine that all leaders clarify that they want to be informed if someone outside the chain of command talks with them or if they talk with that person, but there should never be a hint of intimidation or comments like, "Why did you talk with him without talking with me first?" or "I don't want you to be telling him anything without checking with me first." The days of working up and down the chain of command are over. Leaders who continue to try to manage and lead this way are doomed to failure or at a minimum, to be disappointed in their careers. If you suffer from this problem, *get over it.*

Al, our direct reports and their direct reports learned to work this way over the years, and myself were quite successful because of this style of managing and leading. My direct reports could talk to Al, or whomever they want or need to. As a courtesy they would either leave Al or myself a voicemail with a short summary of the discussion.

Next, *don't micromanage people.* Hire great people, be clear about their responsibility, authority, and accountability then let them do their thing without your looking over their shoulder all of the time. This is a quick way to lose great people!

Shared leadership is a style of leadership whose time has come. All business is just too complex to play those old games of command and control.

There are still a lot of leaders out there who don't understand this yet and actually believe people don't know who they are. This is naivety, as everyone knows everything. The last one to figure this out is usually the leader whom everyone is talking about behind his or her back.

I can tell you that during the crisis of September 11 and the weeks following, I often let two of my direct reports, Erin Wallace and Karl Holz, take the leadership role when they had the knowledge and expertise required for the moment. I stepped in when it was appropriate and when I could contribute most. The bottom line is that we did great work using the shared-leadership work style.

Always remember that just because you have the higher salary or title doesn't make you smarter than your direct reports. I remember Ken Blanchard, the leadership and management author, wearing a button once that read, *"None of us is as smart as all of us."*

This brings me to another thing that I have learned about career development, one that's a strength of mine. It's called *"self-awareness."* I don't know if this can be learned or not, but when individuals are without it, they are doomed. If they have some behavioral or personality traits that are seen as negative and don't ever figure these out, they suffer from a lack of self-awareness and, unfortunately, they just keep doing the same things over and over. It usually has everything to do with leadership behaviors and personality quirks.

This is why it is so important for us as leaders to give people feedback on their performance, including personality and behavioral traits. Some people will never figure it out unless they receive frequent candid feedback. In this area we all have plenty of work to do.

Help your leader or partner give you feedback by asking for it and by accepting it in a gracious way without getting defensive. It may be the best thing that ever happens to you.

There are a lot of people around who have no self-awareness or who are not getting feedback or who are not listening to the feedback. I know for sure that what may be considered a small personality or behavioral trait has ruined many a career, and often the person never even knew why. Can anyone understand how some leaders continue to try to lead in a way that is in direct conflict with the leadership behaviors that we wanted to have at the Walt Disney World® Resort? For me this is on par with drinking and driving, texting and driving or not wearing your seat belt. *It is dangerous!*

Another thing I have learned about career development is to try to do a big hard thing that will make a difference from time to time. For example, a couple things I have done were develop the *Disney Great Leader Strategies,* teach time management courses to all cast members, start the Cast Excellence lunches as a forum for learning, created The Main Street Diary, made major changes to the organizational structure, and so forth. Another thing that is a cousin to this is to pick one, two, or three things that interest you and become known for them.

Three things that I have developed expertise in, outside of my normal duties, are time-management, leadership, and service management. I have a thriving business today based upon my expertise in these three areas.

No matter what field or area I might want to spend time in, these three things offer great value to me as a leader. People actually think I am an expert in these three areas and you know what, I am because I have spent years and years reading, studying, going to classes, teaching, and practicing these three subjects myself. *If you focus on something long enough, you can become the known expert in it.* I have also focused on learning to be an effective communicator through storytelling, and I hope you will agree that I have achieved some level of success in that endeavor. I did not begin to focus on these things until 1980 when I was 36 years old, so it is never too late. Colonel Sanders didn't start Kentucky Fried Chicken until he was retired and 69 years old. The world is full of examples of late starters who made a huge difference in their area of focus. You can do this too in small or large ways if you think about it and focus on it. It will broaden your future opportunities as well.

Remember, *the more you know, the more you are worth.* That's the reason they say, "Knowledge is power." I might also add that, "Shared knowledge is even more powerful." Share the things you know with others. This is called teaching.

There are too many people in business who think that keeping knowledge to themselves is power. You can see what happened when the FBI and CIA did not share information with each other about the knowledge they had surrounding terrorist movements that may have resulted in the events of 9/11.

I assure you that there was not an environment in place where people felt free to speak up until a woman from the FBI had the courage to write a letter to the Director of the FBI about the lack of follow-up and follow-through on things that her office and her supervisors knew. She showed real leadership and courage by stepping up and doing the right thing. I think I will send the *Disney Great Leader Strategies* to the heads of those two agencies. What do you think?

Another thing I have learned is to be flexible and not try to win every battle. There is a time to let things go and see how they work out. Save some of your bullets for the big battles. Don't fall on your sword for every issue. Most things can be reversed later if they don't work out. Nobody likes to work with someone who always has to win no matter what. A good way to practice this is while playing hide-and-go-seek or other games with children, let them win—not all of the time but most of the time—until they are old enough to be competitive. Don't use your position and salary to win, use it to teach and influence others for good.

Another thing that I learned later in my career is to block time on your calendar to "think." Go to the library or to some other quiet place for a minimum of 4 hours or even longer and just think about what you should be focusing on in your life. This is called "time to muse."

And lastly, *some really important things* that I have learned along the way that I would like to share with you:

- Always be out of town on moving day.

- Jump in the pool with your clothes on to really scare the kids when you are playing chase. I have learned when playing with children they love to be scared and to get wet. Why, I have no idea. They like to scream too. Priscilla's niece, Kate taught me this.

- Have friends of all ages, backgrounds, religions and cultures.

- Help your family and friends as much as you can.

- Children spilling their milk is not a federal offense— that's why they invented paper towels. Be gentle with children.

- Spilling a glass of red wine on a white carpet is a federal offense. Your wife will not forgive you.

- Make your boss look good.

- Give credit where credit is due. Practice appreciation, recognition and encouragement (A.R.E.).

- Don't take yourself too seriously (humor is a good thing).

- Don't fall in love with your title unless it's grandfather or something like that (you know what I mean).

- Don't get personal. Keep it professional.

- Take tough assignments. You have more to gain from them in the long run.

- Call or write your mom often (or text her in this day

and age).

- Bring solutions and not problems to your leader.
- Brag about your children and grandchildren, and make people look at pictures of them.
- Use your authority to do good things.
- Listen more and talk less.
- Experience things just to experience them
- Find ways to tell people how much you appreciate them, including your leaders, your spouse or partner, and children.
- Laugh, cry, and smile a lot.
- Put IOU's in those plastic Easter eggs for your grandchildren or children such as a trip to the bookstore or a pancake breakfast or a trip to the Apple Store.
- Give your grandchildren candy after they eat their breakfast, even if it is 6:30am. Make sure their parents are still asleep.
- Don't blame others for the predicaments you get yourself into.
- Wear little, pointed, paper hats at family birthday parties and always have balloons.
- Know what you are good at and do that most of the time.
- Don't use your position to try to intimidate people. Your position is intimidating enough already.
- Don't give up too soon.

- Wear you seatbelt.
- Don't do anything when you are driving, except drive (don't text, drink or put on makeup).
- Give gifts to your grandchildren on your birthday.
- Don't underestimate the influence you have.
- Know when you move from persistent to annoying.
- Don't tell jokes or say something hurtful and then say I was kidding. It's too late.
- Be candid, but with finesse.
- Don't let your kids watch television or play on their computers or phones if they have school tomorrow. They will turn out to be better readers, which convert to better students and better adults.
- Remember that much of what you believe is not true. Take a hard look at your deepest beliefs.
- Don't hurt people's feelings.
- Don't push your direct reports around. They will get you fired.
- Play games with children and watch cartoons with them.
- *Never* say never.
- Use the word "no" sparingly
- Seek the truth! All stories sound right in isolation.
- Tell people whom you appreciate that you appreciate them … often.

- Tell people whom you love that you love them … often.

- Do hard things and life becomes easier. Do easy things only and life gets harder.

- It's never too late to get better.

That's enough for now! I told you that I would tell you how everything has come together in my career and how I now think about all of those ups and downs and aches and pains I have had over the years. I want you to know that each of them was important in getting me to where I am today.

- If I had not dropped out of college, I would not have gone into the Army at Fort Poke, Louisiana.

- If I had not gone into the Army, I would not have met Terrance Biggs in cook's school who recommended that I go to Washington, D.C., with him to get a job at the Washington Hilton after we got out of the Army. Also I would not have met Graham Cromack in the Army. We later became roommates in Washington, D.C., before he returned to the UK. I recently reconnected with him through Google and found out he was living in Spain.

- If I had not gone to the Washington Hilton, I would not have started to gain the experience that has taught me so much over the years and prepared me for each promotion I received. That first job was like the foundation of a building. Each experience after that built upon the last. I am now a 24-story building, so to speak … or maybe even higher.

- If I had not gone to the Washington Hilton, I would not have met Priscilla, and we would not have fallen in love and gotten married. Also if I had not been persistent, we would not be married now either.

- If we had not gotten married, we would not have our son, Daniel.

- If I had not accepted that low-paying clerk's job in the food control office in Washington and given up my lucrative job as a banquet server, I wouldn't have become a manager and been promoted to Chicago where Daniel was born.

- If I had not gone to Chicago, I would not have had enough experience to be promoted to The Waldorf Astoria in New York. If I had not gone there, I would not have had a leader like Gene Scanlan, who took me under his wing, mentored me and then promoted me to assistant director of food and beverage for the most famous hotel in the world. By doing good work at The Waldorf, I received a promotion to executive assistant manager and director of food and beverage of the Tarrytown Hilton.

- If I had not gone there and had a negative relationship problem with my boss, I would not have ended up at the Los Angeles Hilton as director of food and beverage. If I had not had another leader whom I did not learn anything from or respect, then I would have not quit and gone to that hotel in Lancaster, Pennsylvania, where I got fired 90 days later and learned a good life lesson.

- If I had not been fired in Lancaster, I would not have ended up with a great career at Marriott for 17 years.

- If I had not had some political relationship problems late in my career at Marriott and been passed over for a promotion, I would not have ended up in Springfield, Massachusetts, as a hotel general manager.

- If I had not done a great job in Springfield, I would not have accepted the job with Disney as director of food and beverage in Paris.

- If I had not gone to Paris, my son would not have come to France after graduating from college and that means that he would not have met Valerie. If he had not met Valerie, I would have missed out on the three biggest and most important promotions of my life, which was the promotion to grandfather in 1995, 1998, and 2001.

- And finally, if all of these things had not happened to me in the exact order they did, I would not have ended up at the Walt Disney World® Resort in the best role I ever had ... except for husband, father, father-in-law, and grandfather, of course. Ultimately, I wouldn't have gained the experience and credibility to write four books and start my own company.

This is the first time in my life that I am totally satisfied with what I am doing. I am lucky. I consider myself blessed to be working with so many professionals around the world in my business. Someone recently asked me to describe my life in one word. That word is *"complete!"*

It took a while to get here, and there were some obstacles and barriers along the way, but I did it my way and you need to also. Best advice ever, *"Do it your way—and don't ever give up!"*

See the graph on the next page that shows what the Big Career/ Life Roller Coaster looked like for me. This ride has been over 72 years long so far. As you can see, there have been many thrilling and scary rides since the ride first launched! Good luck to all of you as you take your own ride.

Lee's Career and Life Roller Coaster

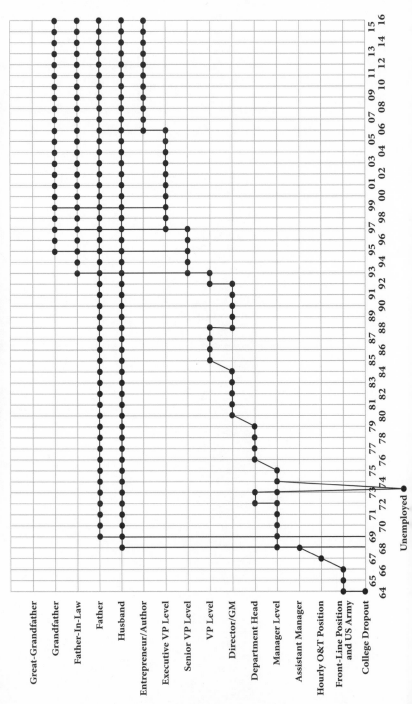

LEE COCKERELL
RESOURCES

Great leaders look for the better way, every day!

GO TO **www.LeeCockerell.com** for additional resources on leadership, management and service excellence, including my *Creating Magic—Leadership & Coaching on the Go!* app, *Lessons in Leadership Blog* and my books, *Creating Magic: 10 Common Sense Leadership Strategies from a Life at Disney, The Customer Rules: The 39 Essential Rules for Delivering Sensational Customer Service,* and *Time Management Magic: How to Get More Done Every Day, Move from Surviving to Thriving. My weekly 15 minute Creating Disney Magic Podcast available on iTunes, Stitcher Radio, iHeart Radio and my website at: **www.LeeCockerell.com** and at a special free telephone number at 701-719-9888.*

There is a wealth of information available to assist you in strengthening your leadership skills. Study and read about leadership and management every day. The more you put in your mind about this subject, the more resources you will have to call on when you are faced with difficult issues to solve in your life.

To experience powerful, engaging and continual ongoing education from me, NBA Hall of Fame basketball player David Robinson and countless millionaires, everyday success stories and time management masters, visit *www.Thrive15.com*.

When logging onto Thrive15.com, enter the promo code MAGIC to receive your 30-day trial to the most engaging online classroom ever created for business people. And remember, when you sign up, an armed services veteran gets a free membership.

Could you use an edge for your job or career? Get a leg up by learning from the personal stories and reflections of the world's top leaders in sports and business at *www.TheSportsMindInstitute.com*.

Please contact Lee Cockerell at Lee@LeeCockerell.com for keynote addresses, workshops, consulting, executive coaching, and seminars on leadership, management and world-class customer service. Phone: 407-908-2118.

About The Author

Lee Cockerell is the former Executive Vice President of Operations for the Walt Disney World® Resort. As the Senior Operating Executive for ten years Lee led a team of 40,000 Cast Members and was responsible for the operations of 20 resort hotels, 4 theme parks, 2 water parks, a shopping & entertainment village and the ESPN sports and recreation complex in addition to the ancillary operations which supported the number one vacation destination in the world.

One of Lee's major and lasting legacies was the creation of Disney Great Leader Strategies which was used to train and develop the 7000 leaders at Walt Disney World.® Lee has held various executive positions in the hospitality and entertainment business with Hilton Hotels for 8 years and the Marriott Corporation for 17 years before joining Disney in 1990 to open the Disneyland Paris project.

Lee has served as Chairman of the Board of Heart of Florida United Way, the Board of Trustees for The Culinary Institute of America (CIA), the board of the Production and Operations Management Society and the board of Reptilia, a Canadian attractions and entertainment company. In 2005, Governor Bush appointed Lee to the Governor's Commission on Volunteerism and Public Service for the state of Florida where he served as Chairman of the Board.

He is now dedicating his time to public speaking, authoring a book on leadership, management and service excellence titled, *Creating Magic...10 Common Sense Leadership Strategies from a Life at Disney* which is now available in 14 languages and his previous book, *The Customer Rules...The 39 Essential Rules for Delivering Sensational Service now in 10 languages.*

Lee also performs leadership and service excellence workshops and consulting for organizations around the world and spoke on behalf of the Disney Institute for ten years , .

Lee has received the following awards:

- *Golden Chain Award for Outstanding leadership and business performance from the Multi-Unit Foodservice Operations Association (MUFSO).*

- *Silver Plate Award for Outstanding Operator in the foodservice industry from the International Foodservice Manufacturers Association (IFMA).*

- *Excellence In Production Operations Management and Leadership (POMS) from the Productions and Operations Management Society.*

- *Grandfather of the year from his three grandchildren, Jullian, Margot and Tristan.*

Lee and his wife Priscilla live in Orlando, Florida.

Please contact Lee Cockerell at Lee@LeeCockerell.com for keynote addresses, workshops, consulting, executive coaching, and seminars on leadership, management and world-class customer service. Phone: 407-908-2118.

Other Books by Lee Cockerell

Creating Magic

10 Common Sense Leadership Strategies From A Life At Disney - Based on the principles taught at the World Renowned Disney Institute.®

Creating Magic shows all of us – from small business owners to managers at every level – how to inspire employees, delight customers and achieve extraordinary business results just like Lee did at *Disney World.*

Creating Magic by Lee Cockerell – 270 pages
Available in Hardback, Paperback, E-book and Audio Book

The Customer Rules

The 39 Essential Rules for Delivering Sensational Service

Lee shares indispensible rules for serving customers with consistency, efficiency, creativity, sincerity and distinction. Lee shows why the customer always rules and presents instructions for serving customers so well they'll never want to do business with anyone but YOU.

The Customer Rules by Lee Cockerell – 208 pages
Available in Hardback, Paperback, E-book and Audio Book

Time Management Magic

How to Get More Done Every Day, Move From Surviving to Thriving

The executive time management secrets contained in this book will help you keep all parts of your life under control and jump-start your personal and professional growth. It's not just about time management, It's about life management.

Time Management Magic by Lee Cockerell – 144 pages
Available in Hardback, Paperback, and E-book

Available at www.LeeCockerell.com, Online Retailers and Bookstores Nationwide